DATA ANALYSIS IN MICROSOFT EXCEL

DELIVER AWESOME ANALYTICS IN 3 EASY
STEPS USING VLOOKUPS, PIVOT TABLES,
CHARTS AND MORE

ALEX HOLLOWAY

This book is dedicated to Meg, who inspired me to follow my dreams.

CONTENTS

INTRODUCTION

Are you tired of spending hours sifting through data in Excel, trying to find insights and patterns? Do you feel overwhelmed by the amount of information and unsure of where to start? You're not alone. Data analysis can be a daunting task, but it's a necessary one in today's world of business and technology. In fact, data is created in huge volumes every day, and the direction of travel is one way: up! Did you know:

- An estimated **1.145 trillion megabytes** of data are produced daily?[1]
- By 2025, the total amount of data created, captured, copied and consumed globally is forecast to reach over **180 zettabytes** (that's 180 billion terabytes or 1,800,000,000,000,000 gigabytes)?[2]

That's why I wrote *Data Analysis in Microsoft Excel* to help you navigate the complex world of data analysis in Excel. In this book, you'll learn how to use Excel to organise and analyse data, identify trends and patterns, and make data-driven decisions.

With this book, you'll not only save time but also gain a competitive advantage in your career. You'll be able to present data in a meaningful way to stakeholders, make more informed decisions and, ultimately, drive business success. If you are a student, this book will help you better utilise data in your studies, come to better conclusions and be able to visualise and describe your observations.

As an experienced data analyst and Excel user, I understand the challenges you face and the pain you experience. That's why I've written this book in a way that's easy to understand and follow, with practical examples and step-by-step instructions.

In *Data Analysis in Microsoft Excel*, you'll learn how to create powerful data visualizations, use Excel functions to write formulas, and much more. You'll also gain a deeper understanding of data analysis concepts and best practices.

So, whether you're a beginner or an experienced Excel user, this book is for you. I'm confident that by the end of the book, you'll feel empowered to tackle any data analysis project that comes your way. Let's get started!

PART ONE
GETTING STARTED

Data analysis can be performed using a variety of tools and techniques, including Excel, R, Python, and SQL. It is important to note that the process of data analysis requires a combination of technical skills and domain (subject area) knowledge, as well as critical thinking, creativity and the ability to communicate the results effectively.

In Part I, we will learn about Excel itself, what we mean by data and data analysis, and introduce the 3-Step System for producing awesome analysis.

CHAPTER 1
WHAT IS EXCEL AND WHY IS IT USEFUL?

 "Excel is the Swiss Army knife of business tools."

GUY KAWASAKI, AMERICAN MARKETING
SPECIALIST, AUTHOR, AND SILICON VALLEY
VENTURE CAPITALIST

Excel is a powerful tool for managing and analysing data. It is a **spreadsheet** program that allows users to organize and manipulate **data** in a variety of ways. A spreadsheet is a computer application that simulates a paper worksheet, where users can input data, perform calculations and create charts and graphs.

One of the reasons Excel is so popular is that it is user-friendly and easy to learn. It is also versatile and can be used for a wide range of tasks, from basic data entry to complex financial **modelling**. Some of the main reasons Excel is used in data analysis include the ability to organize and analyse data, create charts and graphs, and perform complex calculations.

In addition to its many uses in business, Excel can also be used for personal and educational purposes. For example, it can be used to create a budget, track expenses, or even plan a vacation. The possibilities are endless, and with a little creativity, you can use Excel to solve a wide range of problems.

SPREAD . . . WHAT?

A spreadsheet is a software program allowing users to organise, analyse, and store data in a **tabular** format. The data can be manipulated, sorted, and calculated using formulas and presented in various forms, such as charts and graphs. Microsoft Excel is the most popular spreadsheet software, but other options are available, such as Google Sheets and Apple Numbers.

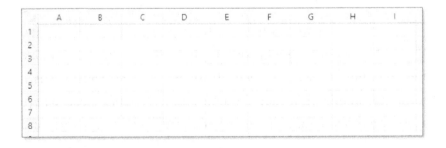

The concept of a spreadsheet dates back to the 1960s when computer scientists at MIT (Massachusetts Institute of Technology) developed the first electronic spreadsheet program called VisiCalc. This program allowed users to create spreadsheets on a computer rather than on paper, which made data manipulation and analysis much more efficient. Since then, spreadsheet software has evolved to include a wide range of features and capabilities. In the 1980s and 1990s, Lotus 1-2-3 was a popular application which has since been eclipsed in popularity by Microsoft's Excel, owing in no small part to its bundling within the Office suite of products and the widescale adoption of Microsoft software in organisations in all sectors.

Spreadsheets are widely used in both personal and professional settings. In a business setting, they are often used to organize and analyse financial data, such as budgeting and forecasting. They can also be used to track and analyse sales data, inventory levels, and customer information. In a personal setting, spread-sheets can be used for tasks such as budgeting, tracking personal expenses, and creating a household inventory.

One of the key benefits of using a spreadsheet is the ability to perform calculations on the data. Spreadsheets use **formulas**, which are a set of instructions that tell the software how to manipulate the data. Formulas can be used to perform calculations such as adding, subtracting, multiplying, and dividing. They can also be used to perform more complex calculations, such as finding the average of a set of numbers or calculating a running total.

Another benefit of spreadsheets is the ability to create charts and graphs that can help to visualize the data. These charts and graphs can be used to quickly identify trends and patterns in the data. They can also be used to communicate the data to others, such as in a business setting where a manager may need to present the data to a team or upper management.

Spreadsheets also have the ability to store and organize large amounts of data. This can be a great advantage in a business setting as it allows for easy access to historical data, which can be used for forecasting, budgeting and analysis. In a personal setting, it can be used to store and organize information such as household expenses, your shopping list or how much you spent while away travelling.

Overall, spreadsheets are an essential tool for organizing, analysing, and presenting data. They are widely used in both personal, educational, and professional settings and have many useful features suited to relevant contexts. With the help of spreadsheets, data can be transformed into valuable information that can be used to make decisions and improve outcomes.

WHY IS EXCEL SO POPULAR?

One reason for its popularity is its integration with other programs in the Microsoft Office suite. Excel is included in the Microsoft Office suite and is often used in conjunction with other programs such as Word and PowerPoint. This makes it easy for users to work on documents and presentations that require data analysis and visualization.

Additionally, Excel has been around for a long time and has a large user base. It has been on the market for over 30 years, meaning that many people have learned how to use it and are familiar with its interface. This makes it easy for new users to learn and for experienced users to continue to use Excel.

Another reason for its popularity is its wide range of applications. Excel is used in many different industries and for many different purposes. It is used in finance, accounting, marketing, and many other fields. It is also widely used in businesses of all sizes and in both public and private sectors.

Finally, Excel is widely supported by third-party software and tools. Many Excel add-ins, templates, and other tools are available to extend its functionality. This makes it easy for users to customize Excel to meet their specific needs and automate repetitive tasks.

So, Excel's popularity is due to a combination of its wide range of features and capabilities, integration with other programs in the Microsoft Office suite, long history, wide range of applications, and wide support from third-party software and tools. This makes it a versatile and powerful tool that is widely used and well-liked among users.

CHAPTER SUMMARY/KEY TAKEAWAYS

- Excel is a popular spreadsheet program that allows users to organize and manipulate data in a variety of ways.
- It is user-friendly and easy to learn, with a wide range of uses from basic data entry to complex financial modelling.

- Excel can be used for personal, educational, and professional purposes, including budgeting, tracking expenses, and data analysis.
- It is integrated with other programs in the Microsoft Office suite, making it easy for users to work on documents and presentations that require data analysis and visualization.
- Excel has been around for over 30 years and has a large user base, making it easy for new users to learn and for experienced users to continue to use it.
- It is used in many different industries and for many different purposes and is widely supported by third-party software and tools.

In the next chapter, we will explore two key questions: What is Data? And What is Data Analysis? Excel is our tool of choice, but understanding Data and the art and practice of Data Analysis is the key skill of the data analyst.

CHAPTER 2
WHAT IS DATA AND DATA ANALYSIS?

Data is all around us. It is the information we use to make decisions, understand patterns, and make predictions. Simply put, data is a collection of facts and figures that can be analysed to reveal insights and trends. It can come in many forms, such as numbers, words, or images. For example, a weather app on your phone uses data to show you the temperature, humidity, and forecast for your location. Online retailers use data to track customer behaviour and recommend products. Social media platforms use data to show you which posts are most popular among your friends. All these examples show how data is used in our everyday lives. In this chapter, we will explore the basics of data and how it can be analysed to gain valuable insights.

24 °C | °F   Precipitation: 0%
Humidity: 57%
Wind: 6 mph

Weather
Tuesday 11:00
Partly cloudy

Temperature   Precipitation   Wind

Day	Min Temp (C)	Max Temp (C)
Tue	14	27
Wed	18	26
Thu	13	22
Fri	12	19
Sat	12	20
Sun	12	19
Mon	13	20
Tue	12	19

24   26   26   22   11   15   14   17

12:00	15:00	18:00	21:00	00:00	03:00	06:00	09:00
Tue	Wed	Thu	Fri	Sat	Sun	Mon	Tue
27° 14°	26° 18°	22° 13°	19° 12°	20° 12°	19° 12°	20° 13°	19° 12°

WHERE DOES DATA COME FROM?

Data is information that we record and store for various reasons. It can come from a wide range of sources, such as observations, surveys, experiments, and measurements. For example, a weather station might record and forecast temperature (example above), humidity, and precipitation levels, while a retail store might record sales numbers and customer information. The data can be collected by individuals, organisations, or even machines. The reason for recording and storing data can vary, but it is often done for simple record keeping, to help make decisions, track progress, or better understand a particular phenomenon. Data can be used for things like tracking inventory, monitoring customer behaviour, or even guiding public policy decisions. Essentially, data helps us make sense of the world around us and make more informed decisions.

Did you know your weekly food shopping list jotted down on a scrap of paper is actually data? You may not be able to easily analyse this data or even want or need to, but you have created data (the items on the list) via a process of data entry (pen and paper) and stored it (the piece of paper). With enough scraps of paper and knowledge of when they were written, you could analyse your favourite foods, estimate when you would run out of a particular item or predict the price of your weekly food bill.

DATA CREATION AND COLLECTION

Data is created by a variety of methods. Typically, these fall into the following two categories:

1. Administrative/transactional – this data is collected for record keeping and is generally essential to the functioning of the business, school, charity, or system in question. Examples would include your grocery store recording what you bought, how much you spent and whether you used your loyalty card.
2. Curated – this data has been consciously gathered to serve some purpose. Unlike administrative/transactional data, it is typically information which is not readily available through our day-to-day interactions as customers or users of a service. An example of this would be a study capturing how a group of consumers felt about a new range of products the grocery store released this year.

How much you spent and on what is available to the grocery store because it needs this information to charge you at the till and to manage the stock levels on the shelves. It is critical to capture this information. However, doing so is also relatively easy as each item is scanned at the till.

Conversely, how you *feel* about that new pizza you bought last week is not information that the store has access to. It can make assumptions about how popular the pizza is by using its sales data, but it can never know what you liked about it and how it could be even better. It is also less convenient for the store to gather this information as a) at the point of buying the item, you haven't yet tried it, b) even if you could explain why you bought it, it would hold up the next customer, and c) people don't necessarily want to publicly discuss their buying decisions with a stranger!

Here are some familiar examples of **administrative/transactional data collection** you may know:

- Computer Systems: Businesses can collect data from various computer systems, such as website analytics, customer relationship management (CRM) systems, and enterprise resource planning (ERP) systems. This data can include information on website traffic, customer interactions, and financial transactions.
- Social Media: Businesses can collect data from various social media platforms such as Facebook, Twitter, and Instagram. This data can include information on customer sentiment, brand mentions, and engagement metrics.
- Mobile Apps: Businesses can collect data from mobile apps used by customers. This data can include information on app usage, location, and customer behaviour.

- Electronic Point of Sale (POS): Businesses can collect data from electronic point of sale systems used in retail stores and restaurants. This data can include information on sales, inventory, and customer behaviour.
- Internet of Things (IoT) Devices: Businesses can collect data from IoT devices such as sensors, cameras, and smart appliances. This data can include information on customer behaviour, environment, and usage patterns.

Here are some examples of curated data collection you may know or even have participated in:

- Surveys: which are used to gather information from a large group of people through self-administered questionnaires.
- Interviews: which are used to gather in-depth information from a smaller group of people through face-to-face or phone conversations.
- Focus Groups: which are used to gather information from a group of people through moderated discussion.
- Observations: which are used to gather information by observing people and their behaviour in a natural setting.
- Experiments: which are used to gather information by manipulating one or more variables and measuring the effect on a specific outcome.
- Document Review: which are used to gather information by reviewing existing documents.

It's worth noting that both types of data collection can be used together and complement each other. For example, administrative data can be used to identify patterns and trends, while curated data can be used to gather more in-depth information and context.

SO WHAT IS DATA ANALYSIS, THEN?

Data analysis is the process of evaluating, organizing, and interpreting data in order to extract useful information and insights. It involves a variety of techniques and methods for cleaning, transforming, and modelling data, as well as visualizing and communicating the results. The goal of data analysis is to identify patterns, trends, and relationships within the data that can be used to make informed decisions and improve organizational performance.

Data analysis can be applied to a wide range of fields and industries, including business, finance, healthcare, and science. For example, in business, data analysis can be used to identify customer segments, predict sales, and optimize marketing strategies. In finance, data analysis can be used to identify market trends, evaluate investments, and manage risk. In healthcare, data analysis can be used to improve patient outcomes, reduce costs, and identify areas for improvement.

There are several different types of data analysis, including descriptive, diagnostic, predictive, and prescriptive. Descriptive analysis is used to summarize and describe the data, such as calculating means, medians, and standard deviations. Diagnostic analysis is used to identify potential issues or problems within the data, such as identifying outliers or missing values. Predictive analysis is used to make predictions about future events or outcomes, such as forecasting sales or identifying potential fraud. Prescriptive analysis is used to recommend actions or decisions based on the data, such as identifying the best marketing strategy or the most efficient supply chain. Some of these are considered advanced techniques and are thus not covered in this book. However, once you master the basics, you will be well positioned to move on to these more advanced practices.

Data analysis can be done using a variety of tools and techniques, including Excel, R, Python, and SQL. It is important to note that the process of data analysis requires a combination of technical skills and domain knowledge, as well as critical thinking, creativity and ability to communicate the results effectively. Excel is often considered the first tool in this toolset with which to gain experience and skill and remains useful even to an experienced Data Scientist.

WHAT CAN YOU DO WITH IT?

Effective Data Analysis is very valuable to an organisation trying to make the best use of its resources: whether to make a profit or simply to have the greatest positive impact on its stakeholders. Thousands or millions of dollars can be added to a business' revenue or saved from its costs by the effective use of the data analyst's skillset and tools. How is that possible, you might ask?

For example:

- Targeting customers more effectively: by analysing data on customer demographics, purchase history, and browsing behaviour, a business can identify which segments of its customer base are most likely to be interested in its products or services. This allows the business to focus its advertising and marketing efforts on those segments, resulting in a more efficient use of resources and higher conversion rates. For example, a fashion retailer may discover that a large portion of its customer base is composed of young professional women and can then tailor its advertising and product offerings to that demographic, resulting in increased sales and customer loyalty.
- Reducing operational costs: by analysing data on business operations, a company can identify areas that are not performing as well as others and make adjustments to reduce costs. For example, a manufacturing company may use data analysis to

determine that a certain production line is not operating at optimal efficiency, resulting in increased costs and lower output. The company can then make changes to that production line, such as reallocating resources or investing in new equipment to improve efficiency and lower costs, resulting in increased profitability.

- Improving problem-solving: by analysing data, a business can make more informed decisions and avoid costly pitfalls. For example, a retail company may use data analysis to identify that a particular product line is not selling well. By analysing data on the product's sales and customer feedback, the company can make a decision to discontinue the product, resulting in cost savings and a more efficient use of resources.
- Developing new products: by collecting and analysing data, a business can obtain more accurate information that can inform its future strategies and plans. For example, a food and beverage company may use data analysis to determine the customer preferences and trends of the market. Based on that information, the company can develop new products that align with customer preferences, resulting in increased sales and customer loyalty.
- Identifying and addressing customer complaints and feedback: by collecting and analysing customer feedback, a business can identify common complaints and issues and take steps to address them. For example, a restaurant may use data analysis to identify that a high number of customers are complaining about long wait

times. The restaurant can then take steps to address the issue, such as hiring additional staff or implementing a reservation system, resulting in improved customer satisfaction and retention.

- Improving logistics and supply chain management: by analysing data on inventory levels, sales, and shipping times, a business can identify bottlenecks and inefficiencies in its logistics and supply chain operations. For example, a distributor may use data analysis to identify that a certain product is consistently out of stock, resulting in lost sales. The distributor can then work with its suppliers to improve delivery times or increase inventory levels, resulting in improved customer service and increased sales.

The answer then is found in *understanding* and *insight,* which leads to high quality decision-making, and this applies not just in business but also in areas from academic research, public health and your personal finances.

CHAPTER SUMMARY/KEY TAKEAWAYS

- Data is collected and stored for many reasons—much of this is to enable an organisation to function, but it can be deliberately collected to find out more about a phenomenon or group of people.
- Data analysis is the process of evaluating, organising, and interpreting data in order to extract useful information and insights.

- There are several different types of data analysis, including descriptive, diagnostic, predictive, and prescriptive. They all seek to better understand the world or make better decisions through the use of data.
- Effective data analysis can have a huge impact on an organisation, whether through the better use of limited resources or the identification of new opportunities to attract customers or develop products, and so on.

CHAPTER 3
THE 3-STEP SYSTEM IN DATA ANALYSIS

Whatever your trade, it is likely the process by which you take an idea or some raw materials to a finished product—one which contains a number of key steps. For example, making an item of clothing would involve initially considering who it is for, what size they are and what they want. Second, you might come up with a design on paper and show it to your friend or customer and get their views on it. If they're happy, you can carry on sourcing some materials, making some initial cuts, pinning the material together and start seeing the garment's shape appear. Next, you might check in with the customer and establish if you're heading in the right direction with it. Hopefully, you've interpreted what they wanted correctly and can keep on stitching away until you produce the finished item. In an ideal world, they'll be delighted with what you produce, and it won't require any adjustment, but typically there'll be something you need to tweak to make it fit just right. The better you know your customer, the easier it will be to get it right the first time, but this takes time and experience and an understanding of what they like, their body shape and style. You might get lucky from time to time, but you shouldn't really rely on luck! Instead, true craftsmanship is a process by which you minimise wasted effort and produce excellent results in a repeatable way.

The process of data analysis always follows 3 key steps: **Prepare, Analyse, and Consider.**

PREPARE

Prepare is the first step in this process. We consider what we are doing, why, for whom and, therefore, how it might be achieved. It can be tempting to consider "How?" first when asked to do something but resist the urge to act before deciding how to place your first step.

An excellent place to start your thinking is with the *problem statement*. What is a problem statement?

A problem statement is a concise description of a problem or issue that needs to be addressed. It should clearly define the problem, its significance, and the desired outcome. A good problem statement should be:

1. Specific: The problem should be clearly defined and focused without being too broad or vague.
2. Measurable: The problem should be measurable so that progress towards resolving it can be tracked.

3. Relevant: The problem should be relevant and important and have a direct impact on the organisation or individual.
4. Time-bound: The problem should have a clear deadline or timeframe for resolution.
5. Objective: The problem statement should be free of personal opinions or biases and instead be based on facts and evidence.

A problem statement should be no more than a few sentences long and provide a clear and concise description of the problem. It should also include information on the scope of the problem and any relevant constraints or limitations. These examples from across different industries might give some insight into what this looks like:

1. Customer Service: "There is a significant increase in customer complaints about long wait times at our restaurant, leading to decreased customer satisfaction and repeat business. We need to find a solution to reduce wait times and improve customer experience by the end of Q2 2023".
2. Healthcare: "Patients at our hospital are experiencing long wait times for appointments with specialists, leading to decreased satisfaction and decreased patient retention. We need to find a solution to reduce wait times and improve patient experience by the end of Q4 2022".
3. Retail: "Our store is facing a decline in sales due to increased competition from online retailers. We need to

find a solution to increase sales and improve customer engagement by the end of Q3 2023".

4. Education: "Student performance in mathematics at our school is consistently below average, leading to a low graduation rate in STEM fields. We need to find a solution to improve student performance in mathematics by the end of the 2022–2023 school year".

5. Manufacturing: "Our manufacturing plant is facing increased production costs due to outdated equipment and processes. We need to find a solution to reduce production costs and improve efficiency by the end of Q2 2023".

6. Government: "The city is facing a high rate of traffic congestion during rush hour, leading to increased travel time and decreased commuter productivity. We need to find a solution to reduce traffic congestion and improve commuter experience by the end of Q4 2022".

As a data analyst, you often will not be handed a problem statement. More often, it will be for you to ask or determine what the context for a request of you actually entails. This contextualisation of what you are being asked to do is one of the key non-technical skills of the role. You may even find that the person asking you to do something doesn't really know why they are asking you to do it! Being able to dig a little deeper and ask around is key to minimising wasted effort. Some assumptions are useful in life—others are not.

Having framed your analysis and understood what you are trying to do and why, **you can next consider for whom you**

are doing this analysis. What we are considering here is *audience*. The person or people who will be reviewing your analysis are typically looking to learn something and then take action. In order for your work to be effective, it is worth considering what your 'customer' can do with the output: are they the CEO or a team leader in an operations team? Taking the example of reducing wait times at a restaurant, the CEO of the restaurant chain and the shift manager who schedules how many staff have to work at any one time have different interests and "levers" (what actions they can take within the scope of their role and responsibilities). Whilst your analysis might lead you to conclude either way that "shifts are poorly scheduled, and we are often understaffed", you wouldn't have approached the shift manager's request from the perspective that expanding the restaurant or moving to new premises would be in scope. The shift manager would have been much more interested in understanding, say, staff-to-booking ratios throughout the day compared to another restaurant in the chain where complaints were lower—as one of the levers they control in the role is how many staff to schedule. They cannot acquire new premises. Audience is an essential consideration in our next step, Analyse, but we will come to that later.

Once you have a problem statement and understand your audience, you can finally move on to consider *how* you are going to tackle the analysis. Here we start to consider the data itself. Specifically:

- What data do I have/can I access?
- What do I need to do to it (if anything) to begin exploring the issues?
- What are the limitations of the data? What can and can't it tell me?

When considering what data you have or can access, time is a major factor. Like the supply of housing in an economy or the range of pharmaceutical drugs available to treat a health condition, the amount of data you can access *in the short term* to consider a problem is essentially fixed. In the long term, (almost) anything is possible. To illustrate this further, here are some examples:

- In a business context, you can only access data created in the company's systems *which you can also then extract* to analyse (into an Excel readable format, in this case). You may also have access to publicly available data, such as industry metrics or any intelligence the company buys and makes available such as market research. If you need to analyse a problem and have only been given a few days to do it, even getting the accounting team to raise a purchase order to buy some industry data may be out of scope. If the company has an IT team pulling data out of systems into a useable format for analysts such as yourself, getting access to data you know is being gathered but cannot access may take weeks or months.
- In an academic context, you may only have access to publicly available data or research available to you

through university systems. You may have been asked to gather some data yourself by setting up a study or focus group, or controlled experiment, which takes time. If your initial focus group's data created some interesting insights, a follow-up research piece is out of scope in the short term and may leave your first set of conclusions clouded by a set of second questions and hypotheses which merit further investigation.

- In a personal context, you may decide you want to take better control of your finances. You could probably access your banking data and download it, but it is very unlikely to be categorised by categories such as "Mortgage/Rent", "Food & Drink", "Car Expenses", and so on. So you might only be able to produce an "Income and Expenditure" analysis the first time you attempt it.

This leads nicely to the second consideration noted above: What do you need to do with the data before it becomes useful? If you are determined to save more money each month, is it enough to know that you are spending more than you earn? How much more valuable would it be to know that actually, your grocery budget has doubled over the last year or that your spending on fuel for your car now that your commute is an extra 10 miles is really cutting into your budget? In this case, your banking data is made much more valuable by taking the time to categorise the spending.

Do you recall the example about the shift manager tackling the wait times at the restaurant? Would it be more useful to have a list of the names, contact details, and booking times of everyone who attended the restaurant last week or a summary of how many bookings there were each day in, say, 30-minute time slots?

Both examples reveal the value of preparing data for analysis as, in its raw form, it cannot always answer the questions you pose to it. In example one, we are enriching the data by categorising each transaction from the banking statement. In example two, we are summarising the restaurant booking data to make it more useable.

The final consideration is to ask what the limitations of the data are? Data is typically gathered with one or more purposes in mind, and its value only stretches so far beyond this purpose. A bank records very accurate transaction data so as to keep your account balance up to date and provides this back to you so that you can understand where your money has gone. Imagine how much less trusting of a bank you would be if they could only tell you how much money they *think* you have and couldn't prove it. However, if you had access to, say, 10 people's banking information for a year, could you accurately analyse how *wealthy* they are? You might be able to approximate an answer using some assumptions such as 'the more you earn and save, the more you can invest', but really you only have part of the picture. Many forms of wealth are held outside of the banking system, and even if you have a mortgage, the balance on your mortgage account only describes what you owe, not what your property is worth. To take this a step further, your current account might only show payments into your mortgage account—not its balance. Are you a new home owner, making your initial mortgage payments on your first home, or are you about to pay off the mortgage and be free of this debt: you cannot tell and do not have enough information.

Another key limitation, particularly common in a business context, is that of data *quality*. If you have a dataset about 1,000 customer orders, you can be fairly sure that you know what was ordered and how much the customer was billed (even then, errors can occur—what if the business was international, charged customers in their local currency, but your report is in US dollars and the exchange rate conversion wasn't performed correctly for your dataset. . .?). A business couldn't function without this information. However, if you wanted to calculate the gross profit on each sale (sale price—cost of item) and someone within the business was responsible for manually calculating what an item costs to produce—how confident would you be that this was always right? Have you ever given fake contact details when buying something online to avoid being contacted with marketing emails? Have you said you never buy a certain type of product during a survey so that you don't have a salesman give you their pitch? What about a time you were genuinely prepared to share your mobile number with a retailer to get postal tracking information, only to miskey it and never hear anything until the package arrived? The analyst's role then includes data cleaning/cleansing— another form of preparing data for use. Sometimes you can fix an issue, and sometimes you must throw the data out. Other times, you have to say, "Only 80% of the data was useful, so the analysis is based on that". Spotting issues, adapting to them and being clear about the approach you have taken is another key skill.

With that, we have covered the main elements of **Prepare**. Chapter Six considers this in more detail, and our example project will cover some practical examples of dealing with these challenges.

ANALYSE

We arrive then at Analyse. You would be forgiven for thinking this would make up 80% of the content of this book. The most common mistake would-be analysts make is thinking that turning data into information is the extent of the role and that they can hand this over for someone else to use. However, what you are really responsible for producing is *value*. This means different things to different people—but you know this already because you just read the Prepare step. What you are trying to achieve, why, and for whom dictates the output that is valuable.

Some people will tell you that a good analyst **always** produces *Insight*. Qlik, the software company which produces Business Intelligence tools, defines it as such:

> *The broad definition of insight is a deep understanding of a situation (or person or thing). In the context of data and analytics, the word insight refers to an analyst or business user discovering a pattern in data or a relationship between variables that they didn't previously know existed.*[1]

Insights can have tremendous value to an organisation, and indeed, this is the most value-adding activity of the data analysis function. However, as an analyst in the real world, you are often simply trying to make an organisation function better, one piece of work at a time. Sometimes, you are just summarising table bookings at a restaurant so that a shift manager can see how busy the place gets on a Tuesday night!

What then is the process and skillset required during the Analyse step? We have our data and an understanding of the problem and audience, so we are initially concerned with discovering the shape of the data—how much do we have? How many rows and columns are there? If it covers a period of time, how many years' or months' worth do we have?

We can then consider more specific questions. Is it customer data? If so, what do we know about them? Do we have their age? How much have they spent? What have they bought? If it is booking data, do we know when they booked? How did they book? How many people are in the booking party? Adults, children? Who took the booking?

We can use our technical skills to explore these questions and produce summary data, tables and charts to begin looking for patterns and relationships in the answers to these questions. Initially, we are both exploring and developing new hypotheses. As we work through the analysis step, our hypotheses become more refined and specific—and along the way, we discard any which prove to be uninteresting or irrelevant.

How then to assess relevance? Enter domain knowledge. This is where the value of experience comes to bear when analysing a problem and is often why it is hard to get an interview or a job offer for a data analyst role (or any role, in fact). Businesses understand the value of experienced staff when delivering their roles, and being able to apply both knowledge and skill is where you can truly create value. Consider again the example of the restaurant where customers experience long waiting times. The following thoughts might occur to an analyst considering the issue. From first to last, we move from common sense to domain experience:

1. When the restaurant is busiest, waiting times are the longest.
2. It can get particularly busy at lunchtimes, evenings and weekends.
3. Bookings in advance help the restaurant plan for busy periods.
4. Last-minute cancellations frustrate planning but create availability in the short term.
5. The greater the lead time between booking and reservation date, the more opportunity to plan effectively.
6. A fixed availability of fixtures and fittings (e.g., high chairs for young children) effectively limits the capacity for simultaneous bookings for certain family types and group sizes.
7. Split-shift (staff member has to go home and come back between lunch and evening service) staff rotations are unpopular and could lead to an increase in unplanned staff absence and last-minute understaffing issues.

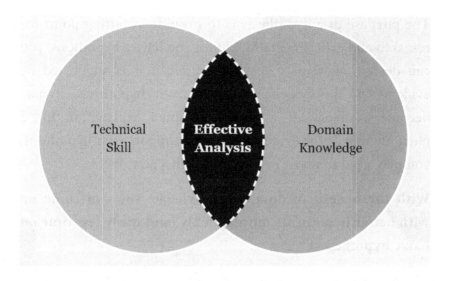

Having both technical skill and domain knowledge allows you quickly (technical skill) and effectively (domain knowledge) consider *hypotheses* that will add value. In exploring these hypotheses, you approach your problem much like a sculptor aiming to turn a block of marble into a chiselled figure: an unformed block (dataset) whittled down into the vague shape of a person (broad stroke analysis—what do I have, how much data is there?), finally adding detail (specific analysis of a data item or segment to gain a new insight).

What do we mean by a hypothesis? In simple terms, a hypothesis is an educated guess or a *proposed* explanation for something that is yet to be proven or tested.

For example, let's say you're curious about why plants in your garden seem to grow better when you water them with rainwater instead of tap water. Your hypothesis might be: "Plants grow better with rainwater because it has natural nutrients that tap water lacks".

The purpose of a hypothesis is to provide a starting point for research and experimentation. Once you have a hypothesis, you can design analyses to test it and see if it is supported by evidence. If the evidence supports your hypothesis, it may become a theory or a widely accepted explanation for a phenomenon. If the evidence does not support your hypothesis, you may need to revise or come up with a new one.

With the benefit of domain knowledge, you can come up with better hypotheses more quickly (and waste less time on naïve hypotheses).

The process of analysis can also lead you to identify new limitations in the data. We previously considered the purpose and method of data collection and data quality as limitations of a dataset. We may find additional limitations through the process of analysis. Imagine an analysis of sales at a car dealership. A comparison of sales this year vs last year to determine what types of vehicles are experiencing the fastest sales growth might reveal that the sales of pink SUVs doubled from one year to the next and that you were able to increase your profit on the sales of these vehicles by 50% over that period! However, you sold only one last year and two this year, which is unlikely to form the basis of a new stock purchasing strategy for a dealership selling 1,000 vehicles a year. The limitation here is that you do not have enough information to draw any conclusions. You have enough contextual data to know that pink SUVs are a very small part of the overall business (only two sold this year) but not enough to draw any conclusions about the underlying profitability of this niche (one data point last year, two this year). However, you would likely have enough information to draw these conclusions about SUVs of all colours.

Chapter Seven which follows, will explore this topic in greater detail and teach you some of the key technical and practical skills used in analysis in Excel by way of our project.

CONSIDER

The final step in the process is Consider. What you are considering at this stage is which aspects of your analysis work to include in your presentation back to your customer. What you include is influenced heavily by what you have been asked to do and the intended audience. The analysis step, in many ways, is exploratory—you are using your technical skill and domain knowledge to explore hypotheses, some of which will lead nowhere. Others will reveal some information of value, but if those findings are not highly relevant to the problem statement or request, then they may not be worth including.

A common mistake analysts make is to think that everything of value is relevant or even that everything relevant is of value. When we consider value in this context, a useful definition might be *'has some positive business application'.* When we consider relevance, a useful definition might be *'addresses the problem statement'.* Thus, valuable, relevant information or insight has both of these properties. However, a senior manager within an organisation may spend as little as 30 seconds reviewing your output and may be switched off by the prospect of reading even an average-length email. Consider therefore is about *curating an impactful message which is both valuable and rele-*

vant. Much like a museum curator, you are only interested in the finest pieces for your collection!

The perfect collection marries Audience and Problem. Your analysis must *address the problem statement in a manner suited to the audience.* A consequence of this approach to tailoring your output might be leaving some of your work unseen and unappreciated. And this is often the most difficult part of the role from a personal satisfaction perspective. However, as an analyst, you are responsible for producing both a highly refined output and being an expert on the matter when questioned. Therefore, some of the work completed—but never made the final report—will inevitably be useful to you when explaining the analysis and the context for some of the individual calculations or visualisations.

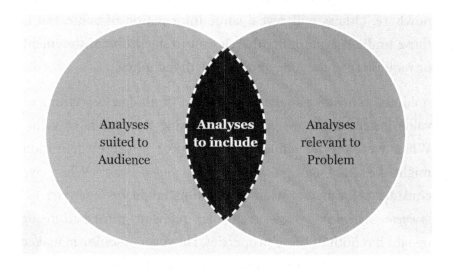

In considering *what* to include, it is of equal importance to determine *how* to present it. Your visualisation of the analysis must be clear and unambiguous to the person consuming your output. It must not ask them to spend too much time interpreting the data or further summarising it mentally so that it becomes relevant to them. Audience again is of critical importance here. And factors such as seniority, ability to influence (levers), intended use (day-to-day operations or quarterly review), data literacy (do your users understand confidence intervals?), area of interest (customer service vs finance focus of CEO, for example), personal taste (numbers vs visuals; history vs snapshot), and so on, determine how you present your findings. This applies equally to one-off analyses and the production of dynamic dashboards, which regularly refresh to keep users up to date on business performance. There is rarely a one-size-fits-all approach.

Let's consider these aspects in turn:

- **Seniority** – the CEO of a company and a mid-tier manager with responsibility for a much smaller part of the business have very different levels of time to spend looking at your work. Impact and brevity are highly valuable to the CEO; a middle manager has a lot more time to consider details and have a dialogue with you about the work and its nuances.
- **Ability to Influence** – this is similar to Seniority insomuch that the more senior a person is, the greater their ability to influence decisions. However, this is also about considering *levers*—what can the person do with the information given their role? The shift manager at the restaurant can give more shifts to staff, but do they have the ability to hire? Can they purchase more tables

to increase capacity? They almost certainly cannot move the restaurant to new premises, and so on.

- **Intended Use** – this is a contextual factor in your analysis. If the shift manager asked you to produce a report on waiting times at the restaurant *with the intention of asking the restaurant manager to hire more waiting staff,* then demonstrating that there are simply too few staff members to effectively schedule throughout the week is valuable. If the shift manager needs a tool to determine how best to use the available staff, then they are not asking you to come to such conclusions (though they may quickly come back to you on this if it becomes obvious!). Another aspect here is that a one-off report allows you some freedom to add commentary to the data and perhaps offer some additional detail in appendices. However, a weekly report which will be refreshed to give an up-to-date view of a set of Key Performance Indicators (KPIs) is limited by your ability to quickly keep it up to date—unless you want or need to provide extended commentary every time.

- **Data Literacy** – this means 'how comfortable is your audience in consuming facts, figures and technical analysis (like statistics)'? Some audiences really want you to take this away from them and explain what matters—others are interested in the detail and will only trust your conclusions if they can see the data in front of them.

- **Area of Interest** – this can be harder to gauge, but a customer who is quite direct may suggest what they want you to explore before you have even begun is really telling you either a) what they think the problem is or b) how they believe it needs to be solved. Others will have no preconceived ideas about what they want to see and are asking you to come up with the answers. For example, if the Area Manager of the restaurant chain is looking to understand why waiting times are a problem at your local venue, they may direct you immediately to produce a report on staff-to-booking ratios, believing it to be a scheduling problem.

- **Personal Taste** – sometimes your customer knows how they like to approach a problem and, therefore, what information they need to understand it. For example, a senior manager who delegates a high volume of their work may want a single-page dashboard that reduces all issues to a set of KPIs and will then ask the relevant member of their team to 'go figure it out'. A different manager might want to see more detail so that they better understand the issue before deciding what to do. This can also be about visuals vs numbers, as people respond differently to alternate presentations of the same information.

Finally, during Consider, you will again encounter the limitations of the data used in your work. Did you have enough data to draw a confident conclusion? Could you defend it in front of a panel of senior managers or your tutor? If doing so required half a page of explanatory notes describing all the assumptions you had to make, would you want to commit the budget to develop this new product, service, or facility if taking the decision was your responsibility?

The process of curating your analyses into a single piece of output requires you to consider the *validity* of what you are putting forward, as well as what and how. When considering the validity of a conclusion in data analysis, we mean the extent to which the conclusion accurately reflects the underlying relationship between the variables being analysed. The validity of a conclusion is influenced by a number of factors, including the quality of the data, the choice of statistical methods used, the assumptions made during the analysis, and any biases or confounding factors that may be present, all of which you will be aware of during the Analyse step.

A valid conclusion is one that is supported by the evidence and is free from major biases or confounding factors that could have influenced the results. For example, if the conclusion is that there is a significant relationship between a certain variable and an outcome, it should be based on evidence from the data and not simply a result of chance or a biased sample.

In general, the validity of a conclusion is an important consideration when interpreting the results of any data analysis, as it helps to ensure that the conclusions are accurate, meaningful, and useful for decision-making.

Thankfully, this decision-making may not be your responsibility, and the context for the request of your analysis may be "we want to develop a new product; give us the *best* information you can on the direction to take," in which case sharing the limitations of the work is appropriate and for a decision-maker to weigh in their own mind before deciding upon a course of action. The point here is that the context for the request was that the business had imperfect data to work with, so a level of assumption and licence to work within these limitations was granted to you.

Thus ends our review of "Consider" in the 3-step system. It could have been a 4-step system as we are yet to look at methods and design choices in presenting data, but this is a topic—or even a book—in its own right, rather than a process for taking a request for analysis through to the curation of a set of valuable outputs. Once you have considered the best approach to delivering the output, you are free to simply do it, which is often the fun part.

LESSONS FROM EXPERIENCE

It is useful, having covered each of the 3 steps at a high level, to reflect on some of the most common mistakes made by data analysts in their work and some of the most useful real-world tips that might better prepare you for working in this area.

Let's have a look at these across each of the 3 steps:

Prepare

- **Tip: You won't always be given a problem statement, or someone will have decided what the solution is and be asking you to measure it.** This is incredibly common when working as an analyst in an organisation, to the point that most of your work may be of this nature. In many respects, this is OK: an operational manager coming to you to support them in understanding their area of responsibility probably knows far more about it than you do and wants to measure how well they are pulling the levers they have access to. It is also OK to be a 'critical friend' to this person and ask before starting, "Sure thing. Out of interest, what's the issue you're trying to solve"? In this way, you are still gathering context and framing the request in your own mind so as to make more insightful decisions along the way. You can also approach the problem objectively and offer new perspectives to your manager. It also helps in anticipating what they might ask for next.

- **Mistake: One report to rule them all.** You rarely have such an eclectic audience that combining finance, HR, operations, and customer service data into a single report satisfies any individual member of the intended audience. Only one person/group oversees all of these functions, so unless the CEO or Executive Group asks for this, you are probably not giving any individual person enough to go on.

- **Tip: Understand early on what the expectations are for repeating the analysis.** There is a substantial difference in how you approach preparing your data for a weekly/monthly/quarterly report and a one-off analysis. The former requires repetition, and in an ideal world, you would be able to refresh your dataset, paste it into an Excel tab and have the whole report update automatically. This requires more engineering and attention to detail the first time you make it, but in the future, you will be very grateful. A one-off analysis, by contrast, can be a little messier, particularly if you are dropping tables and charts into another application to build a written report or slide show. However, do save these workings tabs as people may ask you to alter the output style or for some insight into how you calculated the KPI, and you won't want to redo it—particularly if you can't recreate the same answer!

- **Mistake: Overpromising and underdelivering.** In the context of "Prepare", if you are not intimately familiar with the data that is available to you (considering all of its limitations as well as the range of data items available), you are in danger of mismanaging your customer's expectations. Better to say, "I can investigate that for you", and come back to them with a statement of what you can and can't achieve with respect to their problem than to say, "Yes, I can do that for you", only to let them down. In the time it takes to investigate the data and realise its crippling limitations, the CEO may have told the entire board to expect your full report a week later!

Analyse

- **Mistake: Overly invested in a given hypothesis.**
  Sometimes either you, the analyst, or your customer
  have a preconceived idea of what the source of an issue
  or solution is and seek to make the data fit. You should
  retain an open mind and be scientific in your approach
  to your work.
- **Tip: Start with the big questions and work towards
  detail.** As well as you think you understand a problem
  before you start, there are nearly always surprising
  observations to be made at a high level which can reveal
  further hypotheses to explore.
- **Tip: Sense check with an expert.** In a business
  environment, the analyst is often working alongside
  colleagues who have a great amount of operational
  experience relevant to the data you are analysing. Take
  advantage of their business knowledge to confirm
  whether or not your observations make sense before
  taking them to the Consider step.

Consider

- **Mistake: Lack of empathy for your audience.** As a
  data analyst, you will have an eye for and an interest
  in a level of detail that may be wasted on your
  audience. In a business context, your appointment to
  an analytical role grants you an implicit trust that you
  know what you are doing and are producing a
  checked, quality output. The need to show all your

workings is limited to academic environments where showing you understand *how* to do something is more important. Do not include any more information than is necessary to effectively deliver your insight. Another example would be the use of unexplained terminology or the careless use of language, such as inconsistently referring to the same concept using multiple words.

- **Mistake: Over time, a number of people have asked for similar things, so you decide to produce a single report that could help them all.** The desire to do this is understandable, and it is quite possible to produce, say, a three-tab report that takes the three things you were producing separately and combines them into a single file, saving you time and effort in producing three outputs. This works because the 3x customers are still getting what they asked for. You may also be able to approach them collectively and say, "If I added these two columns to this report, you'd all have what you need—does that work for you"? This approach fails when you confuse what is efficient for you with what is useful for your customers. The MOST common example of this is not fully summarising data that a senior manager needs so that it is also useful for his or her team, who needs a lower level of detail. You are wasting the senior manager's time and asking them to do your job for you by summarising the data to the level they require. Most likely, they will not do this and tell their colleagues that they don't get what they need from your team.

- **Tip: Spend time getting to know your audience.** It is worth trying to understand from your audience not just what they require, but how they like to consume information and insight. This will reveal their personal tastes and allow you to deliver something that has immediate impact. It also moves a conversation beyond content and intended use and allows you to build some rapport with the person or people most likely to sign off your work.

CHAPTER SUMMARY/KEY TAKEAWAYS

The 3-step system proposed in this book ensures you correctly Prepare your data, Analyse it effectively, and Consider what to output and how best to do it.

The Prepare step requires:

- A well-defined Problem Statement so that you know exactly what you are trying to achieve and the context for it.
- The identification of your Audience and an understanding of their roles and levers.
- An evaluation of the data you have available, including its limitations.
- The identification of potential transformations or summarisation that the data may need to tackle the problem statement.

The Analyse step requires:

- The exploration of the data to determine its basic properties—how many rows and columns, its composition (i.e., who or what it is about and the information we have about them), and so on.
- The application of domain knowledge to produce some initial hypotheses.
- The application of technical skill to explore and refine initial hypotheses.
- The repetition of analysis, observation, and refinement to produce relevant outputs to the business problem.
- The discovery of new limitations in the data through use and adapting to these challenges.

The Consider step requires:

- The careful curation of an impactful story based on analysis and observations.
- The effective presentation of the analysis that is clear and unambiguous.
- A focus on the audience and their Seniority, Ability to Influence, Intended Use, Data Literacy, Area of Interest, and Personal Taste.

PART TWO
LET'S GO

Having introduced you to Excel, Data, Data Analysis and the 3-Step System: the process by which we analyse data and produce highly effective output, it's time to begin learning the skills and techniques for real. This involves both the Excel techniques and formulas needed to crunch the numbers and the thought processes and considerations required while performing the analysis.

To make this process as effective as possible for you, we will be working through a project together, using a dataset accessible for free online that has been made available for exactly this purpose. Our project involves the analysis of hotel bookings data for two real hotels located in Portugal. All the personal data has been removed, leaving a dataset perfectly suited to learning some analytical techniques and answering some fictional questions posed by the hotel company's senior management. These questions will help you consider both what you need to do and how, and will be structured in a way that teaches you Excel techniques ranging from beginner to intermediate.

We will start by introducing you to the Excel interface and where some of the key features we will be using are located. This will also be an opportunity to describe what will not be covered in this book that might otherwise look interesting or be something you have heard of in researching Excel or speaking to friends or colleagues.

We will then "Prepare" the data by considering what we have and whether it is likely to answer the questions that might be asked of it. This will cover topics including the structure of the data, its format, opportunities to clean it, and extend it by creating some derived columns (creating some new value based on data you already have).

Next, we will "Analyse" the data by answering some simpler and more direct questions from senior management. These will help you learn some of the more common analysis functions found in Excel in a way that makes them relevant and progressively more challenging.

Finally, we will "Consider" some more expansive requests from management, this time a little less clear on what they want, giving you, the analyst, the opportunity to think a little more about what to include, why, and how to present it.

CHAPTER 4
GETTING TO KNOW EXCEL

Assuming you have Excel, you may have already opened it, clicked around, stared at a blank workbook or perhaps used one sent to you by a friend or colleague or that you found online. However you found your way under the green logo, your first impression may have been wonder, dread or something in between. Here, we demystify some of the capabilities of the tool and help you find your way around.

This book is based on Excel as packaged within Microsoft 365 —the subscription service containing the latest version of applications found within the Office suite. Your workplace or school may have a different version, but 90% of what you will see here or the features mentioned are common to all versions of Excel going back over a decade. In fact, the "ribbon" style of the menu in Office applications dates back to 2007. If you happen to be using an older version of Excel than this, you may find the internet is the best source of information on navigating the menus—however, the techniques and formulas remain applicable. Relatively few formulas have changed over the years, and some formulas which have, such as RANK and FORECAST, have legacy support in newer versions of the software.

A NEW WORKBOOK

Open Excel. You may have a desktop shortcut or the application pinned somewhere to your Start menu or taskbar. If not, you can search for "Excel" using the bar next to the Start menu in Windows (other operating systems may have a similar feature).

The first screen you are presented with will give you some options to get you started:

Click "Blank Workbook", and you will see the following appear:

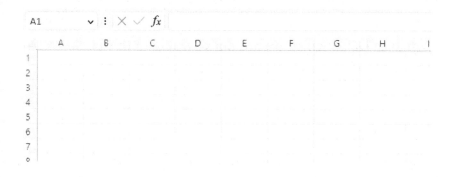

Simple, right? Let's look at each menu in turn.

FILE

The File menu contains the 'admin' features for your workbook —Save, Print, Share, Export, etc. It is also where you could create another New workbook or Open a saved workbook— neither of which closes your currently open book by default.

HOME

Home contains a selection of features used most commonly, so you can spend most of your time working in Excel and only use this tab—depending on what you are trying to do. Here we find clipboard functions (copy, paste, format painter), font, text alignment, number and date formatting, preconfigured styles, cell and row insertion and deletion, filters and a button "Analyze Data", which we are not covering in this book—you'll be learning to do it yourself!

INSERT

The Insert menu contains a number of options for content you can place on your worksheet to enhance its look or functionality. It includes PivotTables, Images, Add-Ins, Charts, Sparklines (mini charts), Interactive Filters, Links, Comments, Headers and Footers, and Special Characters.

PAGE LAYOUT

Page Layout contains options for adjusting how your worksheet contents are presented. You can apply Themes which apply consistent colours and styles to your existing work, adjust the margins and orientation of the page, adjust scaling and arrange items on the page using alignment and front-to-back sorting (what appears on top when two or more things are in the same space).

FORMULAS

Formulas contain a library of options should you not know exactly what you are looking for, each with help and a formula wizard to help construct the formula correctly. You can also use the Formula Auditing tab to show the references formulas are making to other cells, resolve errors, and adjust how and when calculation occurs using the Calculation tab.

DATA

Data contains options for finding, filtering and fixing data as well as grouping rows and columns, which can be useful when worksheets become very large. There are some forecasting features here which are not covered in this book.

REVIEW

Review contains tools to proof your workbook before sharing it (spelling and thesaurus), translation options and the ability to add comments to cells—which is very useful when collaborating with colleagues or fellow students on a project. You can also protect the structure and content of cells within a sheet, the entire sheet or even the entire workbook so that it cannot be edited—or only in a way you wish.

VIEW

View allows you to alter the way you see the worksheet on the screen and can toggle elements of the interface, such as the formula bar if you don't want to see them. You can also create multiple windows looking at the same workbook if you are cross-referencing two pieces of information as you work on a task. Freeze panes is particularly useful if scrolling through a large dataset, but seeing what the column or row names are called is essential.

HELP

The Help menu allows you to access various help features, including an interactive guide and training material.

THE SEARCH BAR

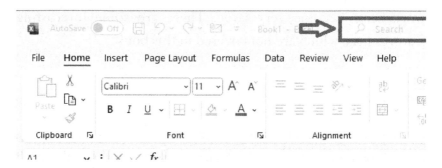

Above the ribbon is a search bar which will help you find features that match or are related to your search term. Give it a try!

WORKBOOKS AND WORKSHEETS

We've mentioned these terms already in the book so far; here's how they fit together. An Excel "workbook" is the name given to the entire file which contains your work—the 'xlsx' or 'xls' (other formats exist too) file you may have come across before when opening someone else's spreadsheet. A "worksheet" (or "sheet" for short), on the other hand, is the individual tab within a workbook containing your data or report. A collection of worksheets allows you to separate and organise your work, whether it's a series of quarterly reports spread across four tabs, a 'data' tab, an 'analysis' tab, and so on. In fact, the number of sheets you can have in a workbook is limited only by the available memory on your machine, a limit hard to reach before a workbook becomes unwieldy. As a general rule, if you are pushing the limits of Excel—whether too many worksheets or rows and columns of data—you probably need a database!

- The plus icon shown above allows you to add a new sheet.
- You can add, remove or rename sheets by right-clicking on an existing sheet.
- You can reorder sheets with a drag and drop.
- You can colour-code sheets as a way of visually grouping them.

For example:

ROWS, COLUMNS, AND CELLS

The structure of any spreadsheet is a tabular grid format comprising Rows (horizontal), Columns (vertical), and Cells (the individual 'boxes' themselves). In Excel, Rows are numbered starting at 1 for the top row of the sheet. Columns are given letters, starting at 'A' and going through the alphabet from left to right. Once you reach 'Z', the next column is 'AA', then 'AB', and so on. The next sequence would begin 'BA', then 'BB'—you get the idea. Cells are referenced by the intersection of their parent Row and Columns. The top left-hand cell of a sheet is 'A1'. The cell below it is 'A2', and the cell to its right is 'B1'.

	A	B	C
1	A1	B1	
2	A2	B2	
3			
4			C4
5			

SELECTIONS AND RANGES

A Selection is a collection of one or more cells which have been highlighted by the cursor. You can select multiple cells by clicking, holding, and dragging the cursor across the cells you want to select or by holding SHIFT and clicking on each cell you want. This second method is how you would make a selection of cells that were not next to each other. Try selecting A1 and C4 *without* using SHIFT and click—you can't!

A Range is a special form of Selection which describes a selection of cells which are contiguous—that is, adjacent to each other. So, selecting 'A1' and 'A2' is a Range. 'A1' and 'B2' is not a range. A Range can span multiple rows AND columns, so highlighting cells 'A1', 'A2', 'B1', and 'B2' is a range.

We can refer to ranges and selections in a formula. Typically, it follows this pattern:

- A selection which is not a range is separated by commas: "A1,C4".
- A selection which is a range can be described with a colon: "A1:B2".
- You can also have a selection of ranges and cells: "A1:B2,C4".

ENTERING VALUES

To put a value into a cell—whether text, a number, or a date—you need only highlight the cell and begin typing! If something is already in the cell, then you will overwrite it (there are both Undo and Redo buttons). Double-clicking on a cell allows you to edit its contents. You can also use the Formula Bar.

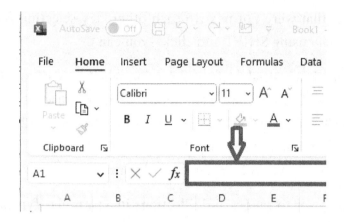

Whether you are writing formulas or simple text and numbers, both are an option. When it comes to writing more complex formulas, it can be advantageous to use the formula bar or at least look at it as you type as the use of multiple brackets '()' are colour-coded, helping you understand which part of the formula you are working on. You also have access to the formula wizard using the '*fx*' button to the left of the bar itself.

FORMULAS

We won't get into any specifics here—that's what our project exercises are for—however, an introduction is essential.

Formulas are where the magic of Excel is found and make the spreadsheet more than a document organised as a table.

Here are five reasons why formulas in a spreadsheet are valuable:

1. Calculation: Formulas can do complex mathematics for you, reducing the need for manual calculations and minimizing the risk of errors.
2. Data analysis: Formulas can be used to perform complex data analysis and summarize information in a clear and concise manner.
3. Dynamic updating: Formulas update automatically when the underlying data changes, providing up-to-date information and reducing the need for manual updates.
4. Reusability: Formulas can be copied and pasted throughout a spreadsheet, making it easy to reuse complex calculations across multiple cells and worksheets.
5. Collaboration: Formulas provide a clear and transparent method for representing calculations, making it easier for multiple people to collaborate on a spreadsheet and understand the underlying data and calculations.

To begin to write a formula in a cell, we always begin typing with an equals symbol, '='. This lets Excel know that it should interpret the contents not as text but as something to be calculated. This calculation extends beyond mathematics. It can include referencing text found elsewhere in the workbook (and even in other workbooks) and useful features like telling you today's date or what quarter we're in.

AMORLINC ⌄	:	✕ ✓	*fx*	=A1+B1

◢	A	B	C	D	E
1	1		2 =A1+B1		
2					

In the example above, the formula is being typed directly into the cell but simultaneously appears in the formula bar. Cells referred to by a formula are colour-coded, giving a visual representation of what the formula is doing. In this case, adding 'A1' and 'B1' and putting the result in 'C1':

C1	⌄	:	✕ ✓	*fx*	=A1+B1

◢	A	B	C	D	E
1	1	2	3		
2					

More complex calculations are possible!

FUNCTIONS

Functions are preconfigured calculations or tasks that you can call upon within formulas. We just mentioned today's date, for example. This is a function called "TODAY". Another one the data analyst uses a lot is "SUM". In fact, we could have used this function above:

AMORLINC ⌄	:	✕ ✓	*fx*	=SUM(A1+B1)

◢	A	B	C	D	E
1	1		2 =SUM(A1+B1)		

Note that SUM is used within a formula (follows an '=' symbol) and that it makes use of round brackets '()'. A function typically contains two components:

- Its name—in this case, 'SUM'.
- A set of "parameters" put between two round brackets —in this case, two cells to add together.

Parameters are *things you need to give the function so it works.* Some functions want multiple parameters, and it can be hard to get your head around what they all are and why they are needed. However, remember the advice above. The function either *needs* it (try adding up two cells you don't mention anywhere) or is *trying to give you a better answer*—for example, a date function might ask you in what format you want the date. Sometimes parameters are optional, in which case there is nearly always a default value you'll get instead. In the case of the date, you may just be given the standard date format for your time zone.

Functions are often given selections and ranges of cells. In fact, this applies to SUM above. It could have been rewritten in two ways:

- =SUM(A1, B1)
- =SUM(A1:B1)

In our very simplistic example, the use of SUM involves more typing than the original '=A1+B1'. However, if you consider a range of 100 values, you can quickly see the value of

'=SUM(A1:A100)' as opposed to '=A1+A2+A3+A4 . . .'. A data analyst is typically considering a lot of data at once and summarising it, so these functions quickly become very useful, as you will see.

This book will teach the most common and valuable functions to a data analyst using Excel, whether in business or study. It will not teach you every function as some have specialist applications outside the traditional realm of data analysis; others are not considered relevant for beginners or intermediate users of Excel.

In the real world, you will encounter problems requiring functions and techniques you won't yet know. The internet is a valuable companion, and nearly any scenario you will encounter and struggle with will have been encountered by someone else who will have asked the same questions you are asking, posted it online, and had someone more knowledgeable come to their rescue. If not, consider being that person yourself and immortalising your query and the answer to it by joining a forum and respectfully asking for assistance! In the 21st century, the information found online is simply an extension of what we know ourselves, waiting to be discovered. You cannot and should not expect to know everything and research and learning are ongoing components of being an effective data analyst.

CHAPTER SUMMARY/KEY TAKEAWAYS

- Excel uses a ribbon-style menu to present its features, with each grouped in the ribbon alongside other related functionalities.
- An Excel file is known as a Workbook and comprises one or more Worksheets.
- A worksheet is made up of cells organised into rows and columns.
- A selection is one or more cells which are highlighted by using the mouse or keyboard. A range is a contiguous collection of cells. Both can be referenced in a formula using the correct syntax (commas and colons).
- A formula allows you to perform a calculation within a cell, dynamically update values, copy calculations quickly across selections and ranges, and allows other users to collaborate on your work.
- Functions can be used in formulas to perform specific operations that are valuable in multiple contexts. Combining functions in formulas allows you to produce some very useful calculations.

CHAPTER 5
THE PROJECT

I n this book, we will explore a dataset and some fictional questions from a business as a series of lessons to develop the skills and mindset required of a data analyst using Excel.

We will be using a publicly available dataset that has been published so that it can be used for the practice of exactly these and other techniques, including some advanced techniques more familiar to a data scientist.

The data we will be using is for a real business, a Hotel chain based in Portugal. The dataset contains lots of records (rows) and many relevant and interesting attributes (columns) to explore. Throughout the project, you will be encouraged to follow along and undertake the exercises yourself, in Excel, using the data for which a link is provided below. In addition, each section will present you with an additional 'Challenge' to consider, which will be a related business question for which no answer will be given. Alongside this, both the method to answer the question and an interpretation of the data will be provided so that you can see if you are thinking along the same lines as the author.

FIND THE DATA

In your browser, visit: https://www.sciencedirect.com/science/article/pii/S2352340918315191.

 ScienceDirect

View PDF   Download full issue

ELSEVIER

Data in Brief
Volume 22, February 2019, Pages 41-49

Data Article

Hotel booking demand datasets

Nuno Antonio [a b], Ana de Almeida [a c d], Luis Nunes [a b d]

On arrival at the ScienceDirect website, you will see the page "Hotel booking demand datasets". This data has been shared under a CreativeCommons licence meaning we can use it for whatever purpose we wish, so long as it is correctly attributed back to the owners: Nuno Antonio, Ana de Almeida and Luis Nunes.[1]

This is their description of the data:

This data article describes two datasets with hotel demand data. One of the hotels (H1) is a resort hotel and the other is a city hotel (H2). Both datasets share the same structure, with 31 variables describing the 40,060 observations of H1 and 79,330 observations of H2. Each observation represents a hotel booking. Both datasets comprehend bookings due to arrive between the 1st of July of 2015 and the 31st of August 2017, including bookings that effectively arrived and bookings that were canceled. Since this is hotel real data, all data elements pertaining to hotel or costumer identification were deleted. Due to the scarcity of real business data for scientific and educational purposes, these datasets can have an important role for research and education in revenue management, machine learning, or data mining, as well as in other fields.

To simplify their description further:

- There are two datasets which we will combine into a single dataset, one for each of the two hotels in the chain.
- Variables are columns in the dataset–there are 31.
- There are around 40,000 booking records for the "Resort" and 79,000 for the "City" hotel.
- There is just over two years' worth of data covering July 2015 to August 2017.

Don't be intimated by the number of rows of data here—the techniques involved are the same whether using 100 or 100,000 rows! In fact, any conclusions we try to make about the operations of the hotel will be much better for having *more* data to work with, not *less*.

GET THE DATA

Use the navigation on the left-hand side of the page and find "Extras". The first entry for "Supplementary material" contains a zip file with two data files inside. Download and extract the zip's two files, "H1.csv" and "H2.csv" (as described above), to a location of your choosing. It is worth creating a folder somewhere on your machine for these files and any workbooks you create in completing this book.

Step 1 – Use Navigation:

Extras (4)

⤓ Download all

⌕ Supplementary material

⌂ Supplementary material

⌂ Supplementary material

⌂ Supplementary material

Step 2 – Click Download Link:

Appendix A. Supplementary material

🗋 Download : Download zip file (1MB)

Supplementary material

Step 3 – Open Download and Extract Files:

Name	Type	Compressed size	Password ...	Size
_MACOSX	File folder			
H1.csv	Microsoft Excel Comma S...	525 KB	No	
H2.csv	Microsoft Excel Comma S...	805 KB	No	

Note: There are Mac-specific formats available within the zip.

GET THE FILE READY TO USE

We're going to combine these files into a single xlsx file as we don't need to separate them to produce analysis of each hotel—this can all be achieved from a single dataset. We're also going to be producing analysis within the same workbook as the data, just on different worksheets. Lastly, we must use an Excel workbook format so as to allow multiple sheets within the file. The 'csv' source files here are single data files—so if you were to add a new tab and do some analysis work, it would not be saved!

CSV stands for Comma Separated Variable and is actually a text file. It is formatted in such a way (commas separate data items from one another) that a machine can read it as a table and correctly interpret what columns to place each value in. Try opening these files in Notepad or another text editor and see what appears!

Step 1 – Create New Workbook:

If you don't have Excel open, open it now and create a Blank Workbook as directed in the previous chapter. If you still have Excel open, clear any cells with data by using the DELETE key. You can clear multiple cells at once by selecting an entire range and pressing DELETE. Alternatively, you can use the File menu to create a new book or use the shortcut CTRL+N.

Step 2 – Open 'H1.csv' and Re-save:

Open the 'H1.csv' file

	File	Home	Insert	Page Layout	Formulas	Data	Review	View	Help			

A1		fx	IsCanceled						

	A	B	C	D	E	F	G	H	I	J	
1	IsCancele	LeadTime	ArrivalDat	ArrivalDat	ArrivalDat	ArrivalDat	StaysInWe	StaysInWe	Adults	Children	Babi
2	0	342	2015	July	27	1	0	0	2	0	
3	0	737	2015	July	27	1	0	0	2	0	
4	0	7	2015	July	27	1	0	1	1	0	
5	0	13	2015	July	27	1	0	1	1	0	
6	0	14	2015	July	27	1	0	2	2	0	
7	0	14	2015	July	27	1	0	2	2	0	
8	0	0	2015	July	27	1	0	2	2	0	
9	0	9	2015	July	27	1	0	2	2	0	

You should see the data appear as above. Sometimes, opening a csv will involve going through a few screens of a wizard which is asking you to help interpret how to open the file correctly. This typically occurs when a file is not clearly separated by commas (you can use custom characters when creating a csv if needed) or uses "fixed widths" to separate the columns, in which case you may need to specify the widths. This shouldn't apply to 'H1.csv'.

The Apple equivalent of all keyboard commands will be included in square brackets wherever required ('[ ]').

Navigate to File and click Save As. Find the location of your working folder, if you are not already in it, and give the file the name "Hotel Bookings", change the type to Excel Workbook (*.xlsx) and press Save.

Hotel Bookings

Excel Workbook (*.xlsx)

More options...

We also want to be able to select and identify the data from each file later on and use the dataset name in our analysis:

Insert a new column to the left of the data, pushing 'is_-canceled' across one column into column B. This is most easily achieved by right clicking on the column header for Column A and selecting 'Insert' from the menu which appears. A new column is inserted to the left of the data and becomes the new

Column A. Into the new cell 'A1', type 'hotel'. Into cell 'A2', enter 'Resort Hotel'. Copy this value down to cover all the rows in the dataset from 'H1.csv'.

A2	∨ :	× ✓	f_x	Resort Hotel				
	A	B	C	D	E	F	G	H
1	hotel	is_cancele	lead_time	arrival_da	arrival_da	arrival_da	arrival_da	stays_in_\ st
2	Resort Hotel	0	342	2015 July		27	1	0
3		0	737	2015 July		27	1	0
4		0	7	2015 July		27	1	0
5		0	13	2015 July		27	1	0

This is most quickly achieved by double clicking on the 'handle' in the bottom right hand corner of 'A2' and is visible only when this cell is selected.

Step 3 – Open 'H2.csv' and Copy Across The Data:

Repeating the step above, open 'H2.csv', but rather than saving the file as a workbook, keep it open as we will paste the data into Hotel Bookings.xlsx.

To do this, we need to select every row and column in H2 except the first row with the titles in them.

Here are two methods:

Method 1

- Select cell A2, then while holding CTRL+SHIFT [Control+Shift+Fn], press the right arrow button on your keyboard. This selects every cell to the right of A2.
- Without altering this selected row, press CTRL+SHIFT [Control+Shift+Fn] again and press the

down arrow. This selects every row beneath your
selection.

- In both cases, Excel looks for the furthest cell in the
direction you pressed, which contains something. It's
worth bearing in mind this is how it works, as you will
inevitably do this again in future, thinking you have
selected the whole dataset, but actually, Excel
encountered a blank cell and stopped. You can press the
arrow button of your choice again to continue to the
next unpopulated cell.

Method 2

- Click on the '1' that is the label for row 1 of the
spreadsheet. This highlights the entire row. (You can
also do this on columns. Holding CTRL [Cmd] and
selecting multiple rows or columns adds them to the
selection. Using SHIFT [Shift] and doing the same,
selects ALL rows or columns between the original
selection and where you click.)
- Press DELETE to empty the cells.
- Select cell A2 and press CTRL+A [Cmd+A] to Select All
(of the remaining data).
- Without deselecting what's highlighted, use the scroll
bar on the right-hand side to navigate back to the top of
the sheet. You should see row 1 is not selected.

Now you have selected all the additional data, press CTRL+C
[Cmd+C] to copy it to the clipboard and go back to the window
where Hotel Bookings.xlsx is waiting. Find the next blank row

under the hotel data from H1 (40,062), select the cell in column B (B40062) and press CTRL+V [Cmd+V] to paste the new data. It should line up with the data above. For example, column D should contain a year and column E the name of a month.

Step 4 — Mark the data as 'City Hotel'

As with 'H1.csv', we want to identify this new data for the City Hotel appropriately. In column A (for the first row of the new data), enter 'City Hotel' and use the cells handle to copy the data down to the last completed row.

Save the workbook again. Now Hotel Bookings.xlsx contains data for both hotels and is ready for use. You've also created your first workbook (assuming you are new to Excel!).

CHAPTER SUMMARY/KEY TAKEAWAYS

- The Project we will be working on during the course of this book relates to a hotel chain in Portugal. The data is real but anonymised and has been shared publicly for purposes such as ours!
- You have downloaded and combined two separate datasets into one to make our analysis easier.
- You learned some useful shortcuts for navigating data in Excel using the CTRL+SHIFT [Control+Shift+Fn] key combination.
- You learned that copying and pasting ranges of data is as easy as text and that the same keyboard shortcuts work for this too,

THANK YOU FOR READING!

I hope you found "Data Analysis in Microsoft Excel" helpful and that it has enhanced your skills and knowledge. Your feedback is incredibly valuable to me and helps other readers make informed decisions.

If you enjoyed this book or found it useful, please consider leaving a review wherever you bought it. Your honest review will not only help me improve future editions but also assist others in discovering valuable resources for their learning journey.

Here's how you can leave an Amazon review:

1. Visit the book's page on Amazon.
2. Scroll down to the "Customer Reviews" section.
3. Click on the "Write a customer review" button.
4. Share your thoughts and experiences.

Or follow this QR code:

Thank you for your support and happy analyzing!

Best regards,

- Alex Holloway

CHAPTER 6
PREPARE

Now that we have our data collated for use in a single file, we can turn our attention back to the 3-step system and begin looking at data preparation. Each of the next three chapters will begin with a reflection on why the step matters before getting into the business scenarios as presented within our project.

REFLECTION: WHAT'S THE POINT?

Let's reconsider some of the key questions which are relevant to this stage of the analysis:

1. "What is the business problem, and what have I been asked to do"? This emphasizes the importance of understanding the context and purpose of the data analysis. It's crucial to have a clear understanding of the

problem that needs to be solved rather than just focusing on the specific task that has been assigned.

2. "Who needs the information, and what is their understanding of the problem"? Understanding the audience for the analysis can help shape the approach taken and the final outputs. For example, if the audience has a limited understanding of the problem, the outputs may need to be more simplified or visually represented.

3. "Do I have /have I been given any starting hypotheses"? Starting hypotheses can provide a framework for the analysis and help to focus on relevant data and methods. However, it's important to remain open-minded and willing to change or update these hypotheses based on the results of the analysis.

4. "How will the analysis be output"? The format of the output can impact the focus of the analysis and the methods used. For example, a monthly dashboard or report will require greater emphasis on repeatability and consistency so that it can be easily updated on a regular basis.

5. "What is my evaluation of the data—what do I have, and what are its limitations"? It is important to evaluate the available data before starting the analysis. This includes understanding the type of data (e.g., numerical, categorical), the size and structure of the data, and any limitations or issues with the data (e.g., missing values, outlying values). Understanding the limitations of the data can help inform the approach and methods used in the analysis.

6. "Which potential transformations might add value to the data from an analysis perspective"? Anticipating the potential for transforming the data to enhance its value for analysis is a time-saving preparatory step. This can include tasks such as initially cleaning, aggregating or summarizing the data or creating new variables based on existing data. These transformations can help improve the quality and usability of the data for analysis and can also help to identify new insights or relationships within the data.

Bearing the above in mind will always serve an analyst well at the early stage of any piece of analysis work.

Let's begin by adding some fictional context to our project.

PROJECT BACKGROUND

You have been hired by the hotel company to support the senior management team with effective decision-making so that the company can meet its strategic objectives. These include:

- Increasing bookings year on year.
- Increasing revenue year on year.
- Improving the profitability of hotels owned by the company.
- Seeking opportunities for cost reduction.
- Providing a high level of customer service and satisfaction.

The senior management team includes a:

- Managing Director, responsible for overseeing all of the company's operations
- Sales & Marketing Director, responsible for growing the number of customers and bookings each year
- Operations Director, responsible for the day-to-day running of the hotels and customer service
- Finance & IT Director who oversees the financial health of the company and has the responsibility for ensuring that the right systems are in place to enable the company's functions to be delivered effectively.

Each director has their own team of supporting staff who are delegated tasks and responsibilities to enable the director to deliver in their area. It is possible to analyse the scenario above and immediately start to anticipate business questions which might arise when performing your role from one day to the next.

First, what are the key words mentioned above that perhaps exist as data items:

- **Data Items**: bookings, revenue, profit, hotel, cost, customer service, customer satisfaction.

What are the declared business challenges?

- **Business Challenges**: growth (increase year on year), improve profitability, find cost savings, deliver customer satisfaction.

Who is the likely audience for this work?

- **Audience**: the role primarily supports the Directors in decision-making. This may involve working with members of their team on a day-to-day basis. However, directors are senior members of the business and will favour summarised data that quickly conveys issues and resolutions.

Why is this useful? Well, you can start to anticipate what you will be asked to do. For example:

- I will need to be able to measure how many bookings there are each year so as to compare one year to the next and calculate how much growth there has been.
- I will need to be able to calculate revenue from each booking in order to measure revenue from one year to the next.
- I will need to be able to calculate profit on each booking, which requires both revenue and cost data.
- If I can calculate the cost of each booking, given some other data (e.g., party size, booking method), I might be able to find some cost-saving opportunities.

- I will be asked to provide measures of customer service. There may be a Customer Rating against each booking, or I may need to find other ways to measure this.
- I will need to present findings in such a way that a senior member of staff can take action using my analysis. This favours the use of charts, Key Performance Indicators, and a focus on the levers the audience controls.

Now that we have some greater context for our role within the business, let's take a look at the data again and consider how we might add some value to it. We'll learn some new formulas and techniques along the way. Note that we haven't yet been asked to do anything by the senior management team, so we don't have a problem statement or any hypotheses to explore yet. That doesn't mean we can't get the data into better shape, as *we have anticipated some of the things we will need to get from the data in the future.*

EXERCISE 1

Let's see how fit the data is in its raw form for answering some of the questions above. It would be very useful to review all the columns of data we have and see if anything is missing. Sometimes it can be easier to read a list of items from top to bottom than from left to right, so let's create a list of all the data items we have available.

- Open Hotel Bookings.xlsx.
- Create a new worksheet and rename it "Data Review". Remember that the plus symbol button next to the existing worksheets creates a new one. You can rename it using right-click and finding the option in the menu which appears or by double-clicking on the new sheet's tab.

- We are going to learn the TRANSPOSE() function, which allows you to take a horizontal range and turn it into a vertical one and vice versa. There aren't any complicated parameters to use, but it does require careful cell selection.
- First off, work out how many columns of data there are on your data tab. The quickest way to do this is to select all of them. Click and hold on Column A and drag the cursor to the right. As you approach the edge of the screen, keep holding, and the screen will move right to show the rest of the data. Note that next to the cursor, a small box is showing how many Rows and Columns are selected. Once you reach the end, you'll see "32C" or 32 columns.

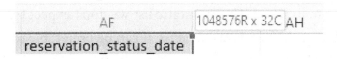

- We need to know this because when typing the TRANSPOSE() formula, we must have 32 rows selected in our new sheet. Let's do that now. Go to "Data Review" and click into cell A1. Press SHIFT+DOWN [Control +Fn] (the down arrow button) and keep pressing down until you've selected 32 rows. The current selection is shown to the left of the formula bar. Note that A1 is still the cell in focus.

32R x 1C	∨	⋮	✕	✓	*fx*
	A	B	C	D
1				
2				

- Without clicking away from this selection, begin typing:

=TRANSPOSE(

- At this point, you need to click back to the datasheet and select that first row of column headings again—the formula is watching what you are doing and will take that row as its input. Once that row is selected ("A1:AF1"), press ")" to complete the function and hit CTRL+SHIFT+RETURN [Cmd + Return].
- You will now see a vertical list of column names on "Data Review". This is a static list we don't expect to change. In situations like this, it can be preferable to NOT use a formula, so let's just take the values from the list and break the connection back to the data.

- Select column A on "Data Review" and press the Copy button or press CTRL+C [Cmd + C] to copy the data. Find the Paste Values button and press it. Now everything in column A is fixed data rather than the output of a formula.

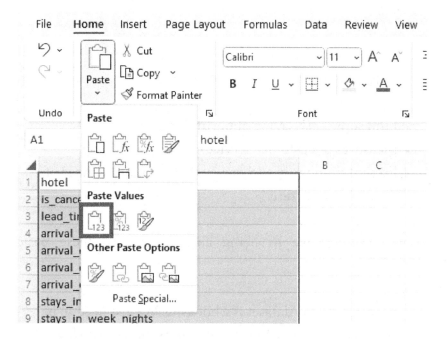

Exercise 1 – Challenge

For some extra difficulty, try producing a 2-column output on "Data Review". TRANSPOSE() can turn a range of cells which contains more than one row or column through 90 degrees. Doing a data review with both the column name AND some sample data can be more useful.

Exercise 1 – Review

TRANSPOSE() isn't the easiest function to use, but it can be helpful in this scenario. Our aim was to evaluate what data we had and see if we could make it more useful. We'll cross reference what we have back to the list of requests we considered earlier:

- How many bookings are there each year?
- Calculate revenue from each booking.
- Calculate profit on each booking.
- Find some cost-saving opportunities.
- Measures of customer service or customer rating.
- Present findings in such a way that a senior member of staff can take action.

How close are we to being able to achieve these basic requests?

- Each row in the dataset is a booking. We just need to be able to count them. We can do this by Hotel [hotel], see which are Cancelled [is_canceled], how many nights they stayed [stays_in_weekend_nights, stays_in_week_nights].
- Revenue is not available in the dataset, but the column [adr] is the Average Daily Rate they paid, so given the number of nights they stayed, we CAN calculate this and enhance our dataset.
- Profit is not available in the dataset as there is no cost data at the moment.

- Cost-saving opportunities cannot yet be identified as we don't know what costs are associated with different booking types.
- There are no ratings included with each booking, but we do know if they were a repeat customer [is_repeated_guest].
- The presentation is within our control but influenced by the data available. We'll come to that later.

So it seems there are some initial enhancements we can make. Revenue would be a useful addition. It might be quicker to include a "Total Nights Stayed" column which adds up weekend and weekday nights.

EXERCISE 2

Let's create a new column in our dataset: [stays_in_total] which will be the total number of nights stayed, either in the week or at the weekend. We'll insert this new column into the dataset next to the data on weekend and weeknight stays so that it is easier to find and read. However, if you were producing a monthly dashboard and the raw 'hotel bookings' data was a system export you received at the end of the month to update your dashboard, you would probably keep all custom columns to one side so that you could simply paste in the new data each month and not move columns around.

A new column in a dataset, based on data which is already in the dataset, is called a Calculated Column or a Derived Column!

- Locate the existing "stays" data in columns H and I.
- Right-click on the header of column J and press Insert on the context menu. This places a blank column to the left, moving [adults] to the right—now column K. You can also use the ribbon for this. If column J were selected [adults], the Insert button could be pressed, and this repeats the same action of creating a new column:

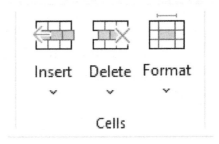

- Let's give the column a name. Click into J1 and type 'stays_in_total'.
- Let's write a formula. Click into J2 and type:

'=H2+I2' You could also write '=SUM(H2, I2)' as we explored earlier. Press RETURN. You should now see the sum of columns H & I in column J.

- Now this is only one record among thousands, so we want to copy this formula down so that it calculates on every row. The quickest way to do this is to double-click the small box in the bottom right of the selected cell. Try this now.

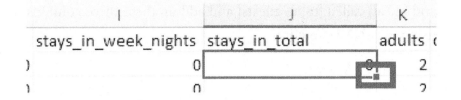

I	J	K
stays_in_week_nights	stays_in_total	adults
0	0	2
n	n	2

- You should see the column update and be filled with new values that are the total number of nights stayed at the hotel!
- Note: This feature works a little like CTRL+SHIFT+ [Direction Button] [Control+Shift+Fn] insomuch that it detects where the data ends and then stops. So it's always worth checking it has done what you wanted, as a gap in your data will stop this from working!
- Should you want a bit more control over this process, note that the default way Copy and Paste works in Excel is to paste the formula in a cell, not its values. You could have copied J2, selected all the cells beneath, pressed Paste, and achieved the same result. The default behaviour of Paste also includes carrying over cell formatting, which you may NOT want. Thus, 'Paste Formula' is also an option under the Paste button, should you need it. This is the 'Clipboard with *fx*' button.

Exercise 2 – Challenge

It may be useful in future to know the total number of guests on each booking. At present, these are split out into [adults], [children], and [babies]. Insert a new column between [babies] and [meal] called [total_guests] and add up these three columns using the SUM() function.

Exercise 2 – Review

You have created two Calculated—or Derived—columns in the dataset. Well done! This dataset 'enrichment' takes the underlying value of the data and makes it even more useful by thinking about a business problem to be solved. In this case, answering questions about booking durations and party size. In the next exercise, you'll see that there is no limit to enhancing a dataset, and we can even use our calculated columns as the basis for further enrichment!

EXERCISE 3

Let's get the data into shape for questions about revenue. We already had [adr] (the Average Daily Rate), and we now have a column which calculates how many nights the booking was for. Our total revenue for the booking will be 'what the guest paid per night' multiplied by 'how many nights they stayed' or :

- [adr] * [stays_in_total].
- This time, we'll create our new column at the far right of the dataset and not insert a column between any existing data. If you have completed both of the Challenges so far, the next blank column will be 'AI'.
- Select AI1 and enter a new column heading, 'booking_revenue'.
- Select AI2 and enter the following formula:

=(AD2*J2).

- This multiplies [adr] by our calculated column, [stays_in_total]. Check that the result makes sense and no error is produced, and copy the formula down to the final row using either of the discussed methods from Exercise 2.
- Tip: Hiding columns can be a useful way to check data when it cannot be displayed on one screen or is otherwise hard to read. Select all the columns between [booking_revenue] and [adr], right-click on one of the selected column headers, and press Hide in the context menu. Repeat this for all the columns between [stays_in_total] and [adr].

J	AD	AI	
stays_in_total	adr	booking_revenue	
)	0	0	0
)	0	0	0
l	1	75	75
l	1	75	75
2	2	98	196
2	2	98	196
2	2	107	214
2	2	103	206

- This makes checking the result of a formula a little easier. Note the 'double border' between these columns. That is how Excel displays hidden columns. Selecting two or more columns which span this double border, right-clicking on a selected column header and clicking

Unhide reveals all hidden columns in this selection again.

- [booking_revenue] appears to be calculated correctly, so this exercise is complete!

Exercise 3 – Challenge

It might be of use in future when considering a marketing strategy to understand the revenue per guest for different booking group sizes. If, for example, all the family-sized rooms are booked out for a given weekend, we would want to know how much we could afford to spend on attracting single adults or couples into our remaining vacancies and still make a profit on the booking. Try to create a new calculated column next to [booking_revenue] in column AJ called [revenue_per_guest].

Tip: We created the [total_guests] column during Exercise 2!

Exercise 3 – Review

Our two new columns, [booking_revenue] and [revenue_per_guest], are both calculated columns based on calculated columns and, again, anticipate further business problems that may need solving. Some business and academic datasets will have all the information you require in their raw form, but understanding that you can enrich the data yourself with calculations is a valuable skill.

EXERCISE 4

We'll create another column to enrich the data further, but this time to improve the readability of the data for reporting rather than some numerical calculation.

The data contains a column, [country], which contains a code representing the country of residence of the booking guest party. Some of the codes you will recognise, others you may not. Either way, we wouldn't want to make assumptions about our future audiences, so let's try to improve the dataset by getting the full names for these countries. As it happens, the country codes conform to a standard known as ISO 3166. The ISO (International Organization for Standardization) website[1] offers the following definition:

> *The purpose of ISO 3166 is to define internationally recog-*
> *nized codes of letters and/or numbers that we can use when we*
> *refer to countries and their subdivisions. However, it does not*
> *define the names of countries.*

Thankfully, there are many websites online offering a full lookup table from Country Names to these ISO codes! You can look on your preferred search engine or use www.iban.com/countrycodes.

- Carefully select just the data in the table from the top left column label down to the far right column entry for the last country in the list. Copy the data to the clipboard.

- Create a new sheet in our workbook and paste the data into cell A1. You should have something like this (after toggling Wrap Text to Off, a button found on the Alignment group on the Home ribbon):

	A	B	C	D
1	**Country**	**Alpha-2 code**	**Alpha-3 code**	**Numeric**
2	Afghanistan	AF	AFG	4
3	Albania	AL	ALB	8
4	Algeria	DZ	DZA	12
5	American Samoa	AS	ASM	16
6	Andorra	AD	AND	20
7	Angola	AO	AGO	24

- Rename the sheet "Country Lookup".

Tip: A "lookup" is a term regularly used in data to refer to a table or matrix of values that gives you one or more new pieces of information about a piece of information you have. You can use the piece you have to "look up" a new piece you didn't have before. Typically, the data you have has to exactly match the data in the lookup table—otherwise, it won't be found. If you have heard of the VLOOKUP() or HLOOKUP() functions in Excel before, this is what they are doing.

Here, we will use VLOOKUP() to determine the Country from the Alpha Code. We will also encounter errors using this technique due to the way the raw data is presented, so we will consider some workarounds too.

- We will create a new column on the hotel_bookings worksheet on the far right of the dataset. If you have completed all the challenges so far, this will be column AK.
- Give this column a name by typing 'country_name' into AK1.

VLOOKUP() works by taking a value you give it (the first parameter), somewhere to look for it—a range (the second parameter), the location of the answer or data you want (the column number within the range, e.g., "Alpha-3 code" is column 3 in the range A:D in the screenshot above), and finally a parameter which is set to either 1 or 0 depending on whether you want an approximate or exact match, respectively. 0 is nearly always the desired setting here if you want predictable results. The one thing VLOOKUP() doesn't ask for is what column to look for your search term (parameter 1)— the reason it doesn't ask is it *assumes it is in column 1,* and it will only *look rightwards from there for the answer.* This means that your lookup table has to contain the 'answer' to the right of the 'search term'. In our case, Country is the answer, and Alpha-3 code is the search term—so they are the wrong way around for VLOOKUP(). There is a simple trick we can perform here, as well as better alternatives to VLOOKUP() which we explore in this exercise's Challenge. Let's do the simple trick to make progress:

- In "Country Lookup", enter cell E1 and enter 'Country Name'.
- In cell E2, type the formula =A2 and copy it down.

- Now Country Name is to the right of both sets of country codes. Easy!

Back to our data:

- In cell AK2, enter the following formula:

=VLOOKUP(P2,'Country Lookup'!C:E,3,0).

- Press RETURN. It should return the answer 'Portugal', assuming you haven't sorted the data.
- If that felt longwinded, try it again, only this time after typing 'P2,' click on the 'Country Lookup' tab and click and drag the column headings C to E—you'll see that this part of the formula has been entered by your mouse actions. Press comma to end this parameter, type '3,0)', and complete the formula.
- Note that in selecting "C:E", we have made the assumption that "Alpha-3 Code" is where our search term is located, as this is the first column in our range. If the country codes were all 2 characters in length, we would have used "B:E" and declared column '4' as our "answer" column.
- Copy the formula down and scan through the results.

You'll notice that some of the results are "#N/A" which means "Not Available". And in the context of this formula, this means our country code was not found in Country Lookup, and so it cannot give us any answers. Let's filter the datasheet to take a closer look.

- Select the entirety of Row 1 and press the Filter button under "Sort & Filter" in the Editing group of the Home ribbon:

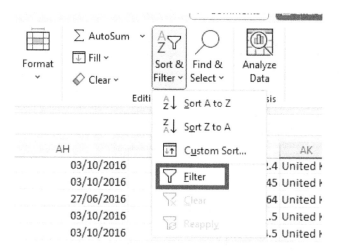

- This will give each column a filter which is interacted with using its down arrow to display more options. Click the filter button attached to the 'country_name' column:

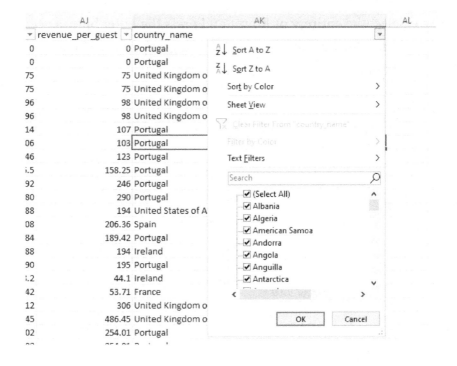

- Type '#N/A' into the search box, and it will appear as the only filtered result. Press OK to apply this filter.
- In the bottom left of the screen, you will see there are 1770 records found from the total. This is displayed just underneath the Worksheet tabs.
- Use the filter on column country (P) to see what values in here are creating a problem. You'll find:

  ○ CN
  ○ NULL
  ○ TMP

- Each of these is an interesting case:

  ○ CN is China, but the issue here is poor data capture. Why was a 2-character country code used here when the rest of the data uses the 3- character standard?

  ○ NULL is a term used to describe 'no value' in a database. This is not the same as zero or " " (an empty space) —it is literally nothing. You can't manipulate it (but you can detect it, which is useful). In any case, this means no Country was captured for these bookings, and so we don't know where they originated from. As an aside, in **our** dataset, NULL is a 4-character word we can do something with—but in the original database, it would not be considered a word/text.

  ○ TMP is an out-of-date code for East Timor, which became Timor-Leste in 2002, long before this data was collected, suggesting whatever system categorised these bookings was, itself, out of date. Timor-Leste should be given the code 'TLS'.

Let's finish this exercise by fixing these three issues. First, we'll use Find and Replace to correct the country codes that are not in our Country Lookup.

- Remove all filters by pressing the Clear button under Sort & Filter in the Editing group on the Home ribbon.
- Select the entirety of column P, the [country] column.
- Press the Find & Select button next to Sort & Filter.

- Click Replace to open the Find and Replace tool.

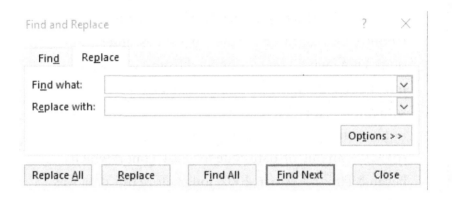

- In "Find what", type "CN".
- In "Replace with" enter the 3-character code for China from our Country Lookup sheet—"CHN".
- Press the Replace All button to update all of these values. You can verify this has happened using the filter on [country].
- Repeat the process replacing "TMP" with "TLS".

Our remaining issue is to clean the NULL values. We can't replace them with values that will make the VLOOKUP() work, so let's consider *doing something with the error* instead. This introduces the useful IFERROR() function.

IFERROR() is a very easy formula to use. It takes two parameters: a formula you've written that may produce an error and an instruction that tells the function what to do if an error occurs. This is also our first example of a nested function: that is, a function inside a function.

- Clear all filters and return to our [country_name] column and formula.
- Click into cell AK2 and note the existing formula is shown in the formula bar.

fx =VLOOKUP(P2,'Country Lookup'!C:E,3,0)

- We are going to put this existing formula *inside* IFERROR(), which works as follows: *IFERROR([some formula that might produce an error], [what to do if that happens])*. Note that if no error occurs, IFERROR() lets the output of the working formula pass through as intended. Click into the formula bar and between the '=' symbol and the V of VLOOKUP(), type 'IFERROR('. Move your cursor to the end of the formula bar and type ' , "Unknown")'. You'll end up with this:

fx =IFERROR(VLOOKUP(P2,'Country Lookup'!C:E,3,0),"Unknown")

- This means that if our original formula produces an error, [country_name] will be reported as Unknown— which is the case—so this is more useful to us than an error, and we may even choose to include it in any analytical output in future.

- See the results of the formula by either applying a filter to [country_name] (look for Unknown) or [country] (look for NULL).
- We've tidied up this data and added a user-friendly version of [country] to our dataset. Well done!

Exercise 4 – Challenge

This challenge is optional but will stretch your application of both the nesting formula and the IFERROR() function. Imagine that, in addition to "CN", there are multiple 2-character country codes mixed into the data in [country] and that doing a Find and Replace for each of them would take some time. AND this step would need to be repeated every time you refreshed your data. Time-consuming!

Go back to [country] and replace all "CHN" with "CN" to take the data back to its original state. Alter your [country_name] formula and update it as follows:

- Formula initially looks for a 3-character code to lookup country name.
- If this fails, look for a 2-character code to lookup country name.
- If this fails, report "Unknown".

If you can write this formula, you have really begun to understand nesting formulae!

Exercise 4 – Review

We covered a lot in this exercise, but learning VLOOKUP() and understanding some of its limitations is very useful to the analyst. A limitation not covered in this exercise but worth bearing in mind is that VLOOKUP() searches your lookup data from top to bottom and gives you the first result it finds that matches your search term. Imagine looking for the "booking date" of a repeat customer—which booking did you want? Did you even know there were multiple booking records? If you sorted the data, would you get the same result a second time? Understanding both your data and this limitation can help mitigate any risks in your analysis.

It is worth mentioning here too, that if you use a version of Excel from 2021 or later (including Microsoft 365), a new lookup function, XLOOKUP() has been introduced. It improves upon VLOOKUP() by allowing you to search to both the right and the left of your search term range. As such, we could have skipped the step were we duplicated "Country Name" in our Country Lookup table so that it appeared to the right of the search term range. Instead, you declare the range where the results can be found (in this case, the range 'A:A'):

```
=IFERROR(XLOOKUP(P2,'Country Lookup'!C:C,'Country Lookup'!A:A),"Unknown")
```

If you have a modern version of Excel, give this a try! It is a more powerful function and will serve you well.

We also performed two types of data cleaning/handling. One was to Find and Replace values known to be errors. Another was to automatically produce a useful output ("Unknown") from something less useful (NULL and bad data). Note that accurately reporting "TMP" as "Timor-Leste" cannot occur without manual data cleaning. In the real world, a data analyst may be working with systems that have issues like this baked into their design which may not be resolved until the company buys a new system—something which may only occur once every 10 years! In these situations, you can build workarounds into your analytical solutions: for example, the addition of some "legacy" lookup records that would map "TMP" to "Timor-Leste".

EXERCISE 5

In this exercise, we will learn another very useful function, IF(). The IF() function has three parameters:

- A test.
- What to do it if is True.
- What to do if it is False.

Nesting IF() *statements*, as they can also be known, allows the analyst to produce a dynamic output that covers multiple scenarios. Consider the following examples as deployed in real-world systems:

- A car measures the exterior temperature for a driver to warn them if it may be icy outside. If the temperature is 4C/39F or below, warn the driver of ice. Otherwise, do not show a warning.

- An air conditioning system is set to keep a room at 20C/68F with a small tolerance. If the room temperature is above 21C/70F, the air conditioner should turn on to cool the room. If it is below 19C/66F, it should switch off as the room is too cold. If neither condition is true (19–21C/66–70F), the air conditioner should continue with its current setting.
- A website is created to report whether flights are running on time. It uses an API (Application Interface) to get real-time flight data and present it back to users. Each flight has a code which describes whether it is On Time (OT), Delayed (DEL) or Cancelled (CNL). To present the information in a readable way, an IF statement determines if the code is "OT" and then declares "On Time", else if it is "DEL", then declares "Delayed", else if it is "CNL", then declares "Cancelled", otherwise show "---" to indicate no known status.

In each case, an IF() statement could take an input value and turn it into something else based on a test you provide and instructions on what to do next, depending on the test result. In the example of the car, it is either freezing or not—a simple test. In the case of the air conditioning system, there are two tests: is it too hot? Is it too cold? This creates three possible outputs— change status to ON, change status to OFF, do nothing. Lastly, there are three tests, one for each potential flight status and four possible outputs: a label for each of the three known statuses and a label for 'not known'.

Let's apply this to our data and create a more useful output column from a simple input column.

- Find the [is_cancelled] column—column B. Note that the data is a series of 0s and 1s. This is known as Boolean data, meaning it takes one of two values: True/False, Yes/No, On/Off, and so on. In this case, "Cancelled"/"Not Cancelled". However, if we wanted to pull this column into a chart to show the proportion of bookings which are cancelled vs those which are not, you would only see 0 and 1 on the chart.
- To make this more useful, create a new column on the far right and give it a column name "cancellation_status".
- In the cell on row 2, insert the following formula:

=IF(B2=1, "Cancelled", "Not Cancelled").

- Copy the formula down and observe the results. For ease of comparison, try hiding all the columns between the input and output columns.

⬛	A	B	AL	AM
1	hotel ▾	is_canceled ▾	cancellation_status	
2	Resort Hotel		0	Not Cancelled
3	Resort Hotel		0	Not Cancelled
4	Resort Hotel		0	Not Cancelled
5	Resort Hotel		0	Not Cancelled
6	Resort Hotel		0	Not Cancelled
7	Resort Hotel		0	Not Cancelled
8	Resort Hotel		0	Not Cancelled
9	Resort Hotel		0	Not Cancelled
10	Resort Hotel		1	Cancelled
11	Resort Hotel		1	Cancelled

- This provides a more readable output to our audience should we include [cancellation_status] in our analysis.

Exercise 5 – Challenge

This challenge will have you develop a series of nested IF() statements to give the column [meal] a set of full descriptive labels. [meal] contains a short code indicating whether the booking party has booked Bed & Breakfast, Half Board, and so on. The website which provided us with this data gives the following definitions:

Undefined/SC – no meal package
BB – Bed & Breakfast
HB – Half board (breakfast and one other meal – usually dinner)
FB – Full board (breakfast, lunch, and dinner)

Create a new column on the far right of the dataset called [board_type] and build an IF() statement that returns the description for each of the codes above in [meal].

Some of the data in [meal] contains a trailing space (e.g. "HB "). As the IF() statement will strictly interpret the data when evaluating the test, spaces will impact the effectiveness of the formula. Such scenarios can be tackled by wrapping the tested data inside a TRIM() function which removes leading and trailing spaces caused by inaccurate data entry or poorly-implemented system validation. Your solution would look something like this:

    IF(TRIM([meal])="HB", ...)

This would apply to every instance of [meal] in your formula.

Tip: The final parameter of your final nested IF() describes what to output in *all unmet test conditions*. This is where the formula should declare "no meal package"—focus on the packages which are defined first.

Exercise 5 – Review

The IF() statement is an incredibly powerful way of creating a dynamic output based on a logical test. Tests can be based themselves on multiple criteria, not just one column, allowing for further refinement. Consider the kitchen manager who needs to know how many baby-friendly meals to produce for evening meal service: in this case, considering booking parties with babies AND who have selected Full or Half Board is required.

Generally, for an IF() statement which requires many nested IF() functions, there can be a more effective workaround. For example, the challenge asked us to determine the best description for [board_type] from some input [meal] codes. This is remarkably similar to the [country_name] from [country] code example. Imagine writing the IF() statement to convert all those country codes to names! For more complex examples like this, it can be preferable to develop a lookup. Experience and an awareness of the various methods available to you will lead you to understand the best solution in each context!

CHAPTER SUMMARY/KEY TAKEAWAYS

In this chapter, we have learned some essential functions available to the analyst in the context of enriching the dataset we inherited for our project. We:

- Took stock of the data available using TRANSPOSE().
- Created some new calculated columns in our dataset for future use.
- Created a lookup table and used VLOOKUP() in conjunction with the data to improve our dataset.
- Encountered some data issues and looked at workaround methods, including error handling and IF statements.

In the next chapter, we will develop further skills in the context of specific requests from management.

These requests will require us to use both analytical techniques (Step 2) but also to revisit our data preparation skills. Data Analysis is not a linear process! As you have already learned in the course of completing this chapter, the data which is available to you is unlikely to be perfectly suited to the task you are asked to complete. Unless you are able to predict the future, you will be asked questions in your role as a data analyst that you could not have anticipated and will require you to prepare, enrich or extend the data you have to fulfil some new purpose. This process of continual improvement and iteration is the underlying philosophy of some of the most successful organisations, whether business, academic, sporting or charitable.

CHAPTER 7
ANALYSE

We come to Analyse, the second of the three steps in producing awesome analysis. Here we will learn some Excel features and techniques that will allow us to turn our dataset into valuable information and insights. Whether in business or study, this process is essential in creating value for your audience.

At each step, it is worth reflecting again on what you have been asked to do. During the previous chapter, we prepared our raw data in expectation of some future requests. Here we will be given some specific scenarios, and so can focus directly on our audience—senior management at the hotel chain—and the value sought through their requests will be more obvious. The questions posed in this chapter will be direct and clear and will present an opportunity to learn one or more new functions or features and may require us to return to the Prepare step to make further improvements to the data. Remember—the 3-step process isn't linear—you will find each new request or question posed of the data may require you to go back and enrich the data. With these requests being more direct, there is less interpretation of what is required.

AGGREGATE FUNCTIONS

The most common set of tools available to the analyst are those which *summarise* the data in one way or another. These are known as Aggregate Functions. They take a large set of information which is hard (or even impossible) to comprehend at a glance and produce a single number, or set of numbers, to describe it. Naturally, a lot of detail and nuance is discarded by reducing something complex to a single number, but it allows you to begin to understand the data. A single summarisation rarely answers your audience's questions or hypotheses about a problem, but a combination of several summarisations can begin to do this. The most common summarisations (each of which has at least one function in Excel) are:

- SUM. We encountered SUM() when enriching our data in the previous chapter. However, this was limited to adding two columns together in order to create another column that would be valuable to us later. In summarising an entire dataset, we would reduce an entire column to a total. We added the number of [adults], [children], and [babies] for each booking to understand the total number of guests per booking, [total_guests]. You could SUM() this entire column and understand the total number of guests the hotel has had over the three years covered by the data.

- COUNT. COUNT() is another very common summarisation function and, as you might expect, tells you *how many times something appears in your data*. Applying this function to our entire dataset would tell you how many bookings were received over three years, as each row represents a booking.

- AVERAGE. AVERAGE() describes the average value from a range of values—specifically, the *mean* as opposed to the mode (MODE() functions – there are 3 depending on your version of Excel) or median (MEDIAN() function). If you are unfamiliar with these statistical concepts, the mean is the average of a group of numbers. You can find it by adding up all the numbers and then dividing the total by the number of numbers. For example, if you have the numbers 2, 4, and 6, you can find the mean by adding them together (2 + 4 + 6 = 12) and then dividing by the total number of numbers (3), so the mean is 4. The mode is the number that appears most often in a group of numbers. For example, if you have the numbers 2, 4, 4, and 6, the mode is 4 because it appears twice, which is more than any other number. The median is the middle number in a group of numbers when they are listed in order from smallest to largest. For example, if you have the numbers 2, 4, and 6, you can find the median by listing them in order (2, 4, 6) and then picking the middle number, which is 4. Each of these has an appropriate context. For example, when presenting the *most common size of guest party*, it may be more appropriate to use the Mode than the Mean as '1.9' guests is not a particularly useful answer!

- MIN. MIN() gives you the smallest value in a range of values and could tell you the smallest guest party size or the cheapest room rate, for example. When applied to text values, MIN() returns a '0' because it can only be used with numbers.
- MAX. MAX() is the opposite of MIN() and tells you the largest value in a range of values. Again, it cannot be applied to text.

These are the most useful aggregate functions available in Excel. Other applications contain a greater range of aggregate functions and, in some cases, return subtly different answers. How these functions work specifically in Excel is explained here and in greater detail within Excel or, indeed, online. Let's try using some of these.

EXERCISE 6

"The Sales & Marketing Director would like to know how many bookings have been received over the last 3 years for a presentation he is making later today. He just needs the number for now".

Here is the first of our exercises in this chapter, and it is an opportunity to use the COUNT() function described above. Each of the rows in our dataset is a booking, and the Sales & Marketing Director has not specified a particular time period over which to calculate the number of bookings, so let's apply the function to the whole dataset.

- Create a new sheet in 'hotel_bookings.xlsx' and rename it "Analyse". We will perform a number of smaller calculations in this chapter, which don't require a new sheet for each, but can use some sheet formatting to organise the output in a way that is easy to read and follow.
- Add a title to the sheet in A1, such as "Responses to Senior Management".
- Create a subtitle for this exercise in A3, such as "Exercise 6 – Total Bookings".
- Make a note of who the request is for in A4, writing "Sales & Marketing Director" into the cell.
- Apply some formatting to each of these text elements that would be appropriate for a formal presentation. How to style this text is subjective, but your aim should be to improve the readability of the output. A heading tends to be larger than a subheading. Bold and italic fonts can add emphasis or separate a label from a value. Here's an example:

	A	B	C	D
1	**Responses to Senior Management**			
2				
3	**Exercise 6 - Total Bookings**			
4	*Sales & Marketing Director*			
5				

Note that text with nothing adjacent to it flows across the cells to fill the space (in this case, the title in A1 flows into B1 & C1. If something were in B1, the visible text would be truncated at 'Responses to Senior Ma'). If column A's width were increased to fully encompass the title, then the styling of A3 would be a little messier as the underline on the cell would stretch far wider than its contents. Getting the right combination of styles across contents and cell sizes takes some practice—it's all subjective, however! The organisation you are producing your output for may have its own style guide or branding rules you need to follow too.

- In cell B6, begin to type the formula:

=COUNT

- Pause when you get this far and note the number of functions that the auto-prompt offers you—there are eight count-related functions offered in Excel 365 at the time of writing! Each does something different and has its own useful contexts. The description for COUNT() itself declares that it *counts the number of cells in the range that contain numbers*. This means that to count how many booking records we have, we must apply this function to a data column containing numbers, not text. Let's use [is_canceled] as it contains Boolean data: 0s and 1s. Finish the formula as follows:

=COUNT(hotel_bookings!B:B).

- Select B6 and use the Number formatting group on the Home Ribbon to format this result as a Number. Tick 'Use 1000 Separator' and 0 decimal places.
- Add a descriptive label for the result to A6, such as "Total Bookings Over Dataset". Your output should look like this:

- Exercise complete! You have the total number of bookings.

Exercise 6 – Challenge

If you recall, there were multiple versions of the COUNT function. To demonstrate another of these in context, clear the formula you created in B6 and see if you can recreate the same result using the COUNTA() function. This counts all the non-blank cells in a range and, for the purposes of the Sales & Marketing Director's request, is actually *easier* to use here. Try it now. You can use any numeric or non-numeric data.

Exercise 6 – Review

COUNT is a very useful aggregate function with many applications, and if you completed the Challenge above, you can see that these two versions of it give you a little flexibility between them to adapt to the data types in your dataset. No numeric data? COUNTA() will help you. Note that you should understand the underlying dataset a little before using the function blindly. A system which outputs data for analysis that includes '0' for unknown numeric data or NULLs will be counted by these functions—and that may not be your intention! You may need to do some data cleaning first or be able to add *conditions* to your function for extra precision. We come to this next.

EXERCISE 7

"The Sales & Marketing Director has a follow-up request for the presentation later: can you include the revenue for these bookings, as well as the number of cancelled bookings and the revenue associated with these"?

This request is definitely one we might have anticipated would follow the original. The number of bookings alone doesn't really describe the value of those bookings to the business and, being as it included cancelled bookings, was never a true description of the business' activity. So here we are refining the original output by way of more detail and, in turn, adding value to our output and, therefore, the audience.

- Revisit your "Analyse" sheet in 'hotel_bookings.xlsx'.
- Let's start by looking at the total revenue request. Much like COUNT() in the exercise above, we will be applying a function across the entire dataset—in this case, SUM()—only this time, we will be summarising an entire column down to a single value rather than creating a calculated column.
- Under the calculation from Exercise 6, add a new description to cell A7, "Total Revenue Over Dataset", and in cell B7, enter the following formula:

=SUM(hotel_bookings!AI:AI)

- Column AI in our dataset is the [booking_revenue] calculated column we created in the previous chapter. The result of the above formula is the total revenue associated with all the bookings in the dataset, cancelled or otherwise.
- Give the number an appropriate format using the Number group on the Home ribbon. The currency for the dataset is not known, so use one of your own choice. In this example, Euros have been applied as the hotel chain is located in Portugal.

5		
6	Total Bookings Over Dataset	119,390
7	Total Revenue Over Dataset	€ 42,723,498
8		

Next, we must address the cancelled bookings in our analysis, separating the number of bookings and revenue associated with them from our total figure. Here we will learn to use SUM and COUNT with a condition, in this case, "[is_canceled]=1". To do this, we use the SUMIF() and COUNTIF() functions which sum or count across a given range IF a condition is true. Let's try it now.

- Insert a row between "Total Bookings Over Dataset" and "Total Revenue Over Dataset" by either right-clicking on the "7" label of row 7 and pressing "Insert" or highlighting row 7 and pressing the Insert button in the Cells group of the Home ribbon
- Enter the text "Of Which Cancelled" into what is now A7, and into B7, enter the following formula:

=COUNTIF(hotel_bookings!B:B,1).

- The first parameter of this formula concerns the source of the data to be counted and evaluated. The second is the value required upon evaluation in order to be included within the count.
- This formula is looking at the [is_canceled] data and, this time, is only counting the cells with a value of '1' inside—the cancellations. COUNTIF is easier to use than SUMIF because you apply the condition to the same data that you are counting. With SUMIF, you typically want to add up a range of values based on the value of something else. In this case, we want to sum up

our [booking_revenue] data whilst considering the value in [is_canceled].

- Enter the text "Revenue associated with cancellations" in A9, beneath your existing revenue calculation and in B9, enter the following formula:

=SUMIF(hotel_bookings!B:B,1,hotel_bookings!AI:AI).

- The formula is looking again at [is_canceled] in column B, applying the condition '1' (cancelled bookings only) and where this is true, adding up [booking_revenue] in column AI.
- Select your Total Revenue Over Dataset calculation result and use the "Format Painter" button in the Clipboard group and click once to apply the formatting for this number to your new calculation on the row below. Your currency formatting will be applied. This is a useful way to apply consistent formatting across calculations. In fact, if you had double-clicked Format Painter, the formatting is applied to everything you click until you press the ESC key.
- You should have something like this:

Responses to Senior Management

Exercise 6 - Total Bookings

Sales & Marketing Director

Total Bookings Over Dataset	119,390
of which Cancelled	44,224
Total Revenue Over Dataset	€ 42,723,498
Revenue associated with cancellations	€ 16,727,237

- It's useful in these moments to sense check the result. The number of cancellations in the dataset is roughly 1/3 of the total, which is also true of the revenue figure. If the lost revenue was a much larger—or smaller—proportion of the total revenue, it might suggest a calculation error.

We've satisfied the Sales & Marketing Director's request! However, the output could be better formatted, and we've interpreted the request quite literally rather than adding value by including extra detail. Try the challenge below.

Exercise 7 – Challenge

In this challenge, we'll improve the format and layout of the output and use this as an opportunity to learn the COUNTIFS() and SUMIFS() formulas. These two variations on the formulas used above allow for multiple conditions to be applied, not just one. However, you can specify a single condition in each case, so arguably, these are more useful than the original versions for their flexibility.

Alter the layout of your output on the Analyse sheet as follows:

	A	B	C	D	E
1	Responses to Senior Management				
2					
3	Exercise 6 - Total Bookings				
4	*Sales & Marketing Director*				
5		Dataset	2015	2016	2017
6	Total Bookings	119,390			
7	of which Completed				
8	of which Cancelled	44,224			
9					
10	Total Revenue	€ 42,723,498			
11	Revenue associated with completed bookings				
12	Revenue associated with cancellations	€ 16,727,237			

Note the inclusion of new rows for Completed Bookings, the removal of "Dataset" from the row labels and the inclusion of some new column headings. We've also added an indent to the Alignment of the calculations, which breaks down the total to reinforce that these are subtotals.

To demonstrate how multiple criteria are applied, we will calculate the revenue associated with completed bookings in 2015—the rest is up to you.

- Select cell C11 and enter the following formula:

=SUMIFS(hotel_bookings!AI:AI,hotel_bookings!B:B,0,hotel_-bookings!D:D,2015).

- Note the order of parameters has reversed as compared to SUMIF(). We now enter parameters in the following order:

  ○ Sum Range – the data you want to add up—[booking_revenue].
  ○ Criteria1 Range – the first set of data containing your condition [is_canceled].
  ○ Criteria1 Condition – the condition you want to be true for Criteria1, '0'—not cancelled.
  ○ Criteria2 Range – the second set of data containing your condition [arrival_year].
  ○ Criteria2 Condition – the condition you want to be true for Criteria2, '2015'.

- COUNTIFS and SUMIFS can be given 127 conditions in this manner!
- The result for 2015 should be 4,511,559.
- Go ahead and complete the grid. Rename the analysis "Bookings and Revenue by Year", replacing "Exercise 6 – Total Bookings".

Exercise 7 – Review

If you completed the challenge, you should have something that looks like this:

	A	B	C	D	E
1	Responses to Senior Management				
2					
3	Bookings And Revenue Analysis By Year				
4	*Sales & Marketing Director*				
5		Dataset	2015	2016	2017
6	Total Bookings	119,390	21,996	56,707	40,687
7	of which Completed	75,166	13,854	36,370	24,942
8	of which Cancelled	44,224	8,142	20,337	15,745
9					
10	Total Revenue	€ 42,723,498	€ 6,818,117	€ 18,870,601	€ 17,034,780
11	Revenue associated with completed bookings	€ 25,996,260	€ 4,511,559	€ 11,673,501	€ 9,811,200
12	Revenue associated with cancellations	€ 16,727,237	€ 2,306,557	€ 7,197,100	€ 7,223,580
13					

It is essential to sense check your output before sharing it—particularly in a business context. If your professional role is to complete analyses of this type, you are implicitly trusted to get the answers to questions right and to have checked your work. Ensure that your yearly values total the dataset value—select the three-year cells in the row and check the quick totals in the bottom right of the window:

Bookings And Revenue Analysis By Year				
Sales & Marketing Director				
	Dataset	2015	2016	2017
Total Bookings	119,390	21,996	56,707	40,687
of which Completed	75,166	13,854	36,370	24,942
of which Cancelled	44,224	8,142	20,337	15,745

Summary bar: Average: 39,797   Count: 3   Sum: 119,390

Your column subtotals should also add up to the total too.

The purpose of the challenge in Exercise 7 is not just to teach you COUNTIFS() and SUMIFS() but to demonstrate the value of not just answering the request but taking the time to add that extra level of detail that provides both context and anticipates any follow-up questions. The inclusion of figures for completed bookings—both count and sum—if nothing else, stops the Sales & Marketing Director from needing to work out the actual revenue achieved without having to mentally subtract the cancellation data from the totals. Value added.

EXERCISE 8

"The Operations Director would like to understand which months of the year are busiest to ensure staffing levels are appropriate for next season".

In this exercise, we will address the request above from the Operations Director. We don't have any data about staffing or what levels of staffing are appropriate, so our best approach is to give an expansive output on bookings volumes by month and hope it is as valuable as possible. We know our data covers three years of the hotel's operations, so it might be useful to report monthly volumes for each year and present an average.

We will be using the data in column E, [arrival_date_month], which is given in an unabbreviated text format (as opposed to "Jan" or 01, we have "January", for example). As we will be using the month name in our formula, our output should also use the month name in the same format.

- Prepare a grid as follows on your Analyse tab beneath your analysis for the Sales & Marketing Director:

	A	B	C	D	E
16	Booking Volumes By Month				
17	*Operations Director*				
18		Average	2015	2016	2017
19	January				
20	February				
21	March				
22	April				
23	May				
24	June				
25	July				
26	August				
27	September				
28	October				
29	November				
30	December				

- We will once again use COUNTIFS() to populate the year columns of the table, and we will only include completed bookings ([is_canceled]=0) as guests who cancel do not turn up, and so are not relevant to considering staffing levels!
- In cell C19 (January 2015 bookings), enter the following formula:

=COUNTIFS(hotel_bookings!E:E,"January",hotel_bookings!-D:D,2015,hotel_bookings!B:B,0).

- This is counting the number of rows in the data for which the booking was for January in 2015 and not cancelled (E = "January", D=2015, B=0). Note that January is in quotation marks. This tells Excel that this is text and is how a text *string* is declared in an Excel formula.

- The answer is 0! Fear not; the data does not begin in January for this year and so only partially covers this period. In order to complete this grid, you would need to type out 12 (months) x 3 (years) versions of this formula which is time-consuming. So we will look now at dynamic cell references.
- What we want to be able to do is to copy the formula down from January to December and across from 2015 to 2017 and only type it once. We do this by telling Excel where to look for its parameters using a cell reference rather than explicitly typing it out. In the example above, we can replace "January" with A19. You end up with this instead:

=COUNTIFS(hotel_bookings!E:E,A19,hotel_bookings!-D:D,2015,hotel_bookings!B:B,0).

- Select the cell containing this formula and copy and paste it into cells D19 and E19 or use the handle at the bottom right of the cell and drag across to E19 to produce the same result.
- Again, you will have 3x zeros. This time, it IS an error. Click into D19, the formula for January 2016. Note that a number of things have changed:

  ○ Condition1 is looking in column F for the value of B19.
  ○ Condition2 is looking in column E for 2015.
  ○ Condition3 is looking in column C for 0.

- This is not what we want. We still want the formula to look in column E's data for month name, D for year, and C for cancellation status. In other words, when we copied the cell to the right, all the cell references shifted to the right too. Check E19—same problem, but cell references another step to the right.
- **We want to declare the references as fixed so that copying them doesn't change them.**
- We do this by using the '$' symbol, which can be applied to both the column and row parts of a cell reference. Let's rewrite our original formula as follows:

=COUNTIFS(hotel_bookings!$E:$E,$A19,hotel_bookings!-$D:$D,2015,hotel_bookings!$B:$B,0).

- We added a $ to all the column references (E, D, B—the data hasn't and will not move). We also added a $ to "A19", but only at the front. That's because Month (our search term in our analysis grid) is always in Column A, but the month itself is on different rows. So when we copy the formula across from 2015 to 2017, column and row won't change (A19). However, when we copy it down from January to December, we do want the row to change but not the column. "A19" would fix both row AND column.
- Copy the formula down from January to December. You should have this:

	A	B	C	D	E
16	Booking Volumes By Month				
17	*Operations Director*				
18		Average	2015	2016	2017
19	January		0		
20	February		0		
21	March		0		
22	April		0		
23	May		0		
24	June		0		
25	July		1517		
26	August		2291		
27	September		3020		
28	October		3225		
29	November		1854		
30	December		1947		

- Now we can see that the formula is working. It's just that there is no booking data for January to June 2015.
- Try to copy this formula across to complete the 2016 and 2017 columns—you'll notice that you get an identical result to 2015. That's because 2015 is explicitly stated in your formula—you need to update the formula to directly reference the year number at the top of the grid.

You will complete this in the challenge below.

Exercise 8 – Challenge

As introduced above, we need to further adapt the formula so that it dynamically references the year rather than typing it into the formula itself.

- Replace '2015' in the original formula with a cell reference that contains the year (C18).
- Use the $ symbol to fix the reference in such a way that

you can write the formula once and copy it across the entire table for years 2015–2017.

- You have completed the challenge when you produce this grid:

	A	B	C	D	E
16	Booking Volumes By Month				
17	*Operations Director*				
18		Average	2015	2016	2017
19	January		0	1691	2431
20	February		0	2554	2818
21	March		0	3347	3298
22	April		0	3367	3198
23	May		0	3563	3551
24	June		0	3196	3208
25	July		1517	3073	3329
26	August		2291	3238	3109
27	September		3020	3372	0
28	October		3225	3689	0
29	November		1854	2818	0
30	December		1947	2462	0

Note again that 2017 is not a complete year with respect to booking data. We will consider this in how we prepare our Average column for the Operations Director.

Exercise 8 – Review

In this exercise, we understood the value of using cell references in formula as a time-saving skill when duplicating formula across a range. We also extended our ability with COUNTIFS() by using three different criteria.

We've also learned that a tabular format for presenting this data to the Operations Director adds clarity and readability.

EXERCISE 9

Next, we will prepare the Average column for the Operations Director. In any business, a range of external factors can affect operations. A global pandemic, for example, would surely affect the booking volume experienced by a hotel or restaurant. For this reason, it can be useful to prepare averages so that business planning is not overly influenced by particularly good or bad circumstantial factors in one year. It is not clear why this dataset covers a 26-month period, but we adapt to data we have and ask of it only what it can tell us. As an observation, we have:

- 2 years' data for January to June (2016, 2017).
- 3 years' data for July and August (2015, 2016, 2017).
- 2 years' data for September to December (2015, 2016).

In calculating our averages for each month, we should only use the data we have. In this case, 0 is not the true number of bookings for January to June 2015, nor September to December 2017, so we will treat each block of months differently.

- In cell B19, type the following formula:

=AVERAGE(D19:E19).

- Copy it down to cell B24.
- In cell B25, create a formula which includes the values in C:E and copy to B26.

- In cell B27, create a formula which includes the values in C:D and copy to B30.
- Apply number formatting to the whole table, adding a thousand separator and reducing decimal places to 0.
- You should end up with this:

	A	B	C	D	E
16	Booking Volumes By Month				
17	*Operations Director*				
18		Average	2015	2016	2017
19	January	2,061	0	1,691	2,431
20	February	2,686	0	2,554	2,818
21	March	3,323	0	3,347	3,298
22	April	3,283	0	3,367	3,198
23	May	3,557	0	3,563	3,551
24	June	3,202	0	3,196	3,208
25	July	2,640	1,517	3,073	3,329
26	August	2,879	2,291	3,238	3,109
27	September	3,196	3,020	3,372	0
28	October	3,457	3,225	3,689	0
29	November	2,336	1,854	2,818	0
30	December	2,205	1,947	2,462	0

- Let's improve the readability of this table by adding some formatting to highlight the busiest months. We will use a helpful feature called Conditional Formatting. Conditional Formatting is a powerful tool which enhances the readability and value of an output by highlighting the key areas of concern or opportunity in an otherwise hard-to-read table of numbers. You can do a lot with Conditional Formatting, but we will just look at a simple use case in this book. Select your Average data (B19:B30) and press the Conditional Formatting button in the Styles group on the Home ribbon:

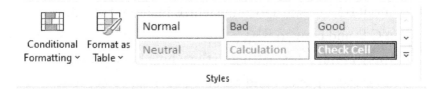

- From the drop-down which appears, select 'Color Scales' and the option "Red – White – Green Color Scale", which is the top right option presented. Excel will apply the following formatting to your Average data:

Booking Volumes By Month

Operations Director

	Average	2015	2016	2017
January	2,061	0	1,691	2,431
February	2,686	0	2,554	2,818
March	3,323	0	3,347	3,298
April	3,283	0	3,367	3,198
May	3,557	0	3,563	3,551
June	3,202	0	3,196	3,208
July	2,640	1,517	3,073	3,329
August	2,879	2,291	3,238	3,109
September	3,196	3,020	3,372	0
October	3,457	3,225	3,689	0
November	2,336	1,854	2,818	0
December	2,205	1,947	2,462	0

- Now, the Operations Director can see at a glance that the busiest month is May, followed by October, with several months of a similar level following that (March, April, June, and September).
- Let's complete the output by adding an explanatory note just beneath: someone reading this output might not understand what the data is and is not showing. In cell A32, add the following text:

- "Data excludes cancelled bookings. Averages do not include months where no data was available".

With that, you have satisfied the Director's request and produced an output that goes above and beyond. A year-by-year context is provided, and the Average column—not requested—is an application of business knowledge: that there are annual fluctuations for various reasons, and so reducing the 'noise' in the data reveals the underlying pattern.

Exercise 9 – Challenge

Our calculation of the Average column data was a little clunky. We had to effectively write three different formulas: one for each of the permutations of what underlying booking data was available.

This challenge will get you to revisit your knowledge of the IF() statement and combine it with AVERAGE(). Write a single formula to copy down the entire Average column that uses IF and AVERAGE

Tip: It can help to think about a problem using something known as *pseudocode*. This involves writing down what you want to achieve in plain English and then trying to turn it into code, or in this case, an Excel formula. To get you started, think about the problem this way:

- If I have no 2015 data, then average 2016 and 2017.
- If I have no 2017 data, then average 2015 and 2016.
- Otherwise, average 2015–2017.

This is also achievable using the AVERAGEIF() function—look at the parameters the function takes and consider what criterion would produce the same result. You could even simply delete all the zero values from the cells.

However, you need to be able to handle any situation. What if the data was refreshed and, suddenly, we had bookings for September 2017? Now any cell where you cleared the formula won't update. What if, rather than 0s, some months had a low number of bookings due to renovations at the hotel, and you wanted to exclude any month in a given year with fewer than 500 bookings as "not representative of regular trading"? Understanding how to combine functions gives you this extra control.

Good luck, and check that you have the same result at the end!

Exercise 9 – Review

In this exercise, we learned how to use cell references in formulas and to use the $ symbol to "fix" formulas in place to enable copying across ranges. We also used Conditional Formatting to make an output easier to read—it also answered the Director's question (*"which months are busiest"*) without taking away the valuable contextual information in the table—though you can have too much of a good thing.

If you completed the challenge, you created a more complex formula in order to handle imperfect data.

Did anything surprise you about the results of the analysis? Portugal is a popular destination during summer months due to its pleasant climate and coastline. Would it have made more sense for the busiest periods to be concentrated in summer months? We do have two hotel types in our dataset, the Resort Hotel and the City Hotel. It could be that if these were separated in our analysis, we would find different booking patterns between the two.

EXERCISE 10

"The Operations Director would like to introduce a new customer service metric: '% Bookings Made By Previous Customers' and understand the performance of this metric over the last 3 years".

In this exercise, we will develop a new Key Performance Indicator (KPI) for the business, calculate it, and then present the KPI across a number of time periods that will allow the Director to understand the hotel's performance against it. Many KPIs are expressed as percentages, rates or ratios as they summarise performance into a single number. They usually express growth (e.g., profit, revenue, cost), proportions (e.g., staff/customer ratio, % orders by repeat customers) or ratings (e.g., average customer review). Alongside the actual calculated performance of KPI, an organisation often has a target—a level of performance they wish to achieve strategically—and reporting both the KPI itself AND its performance against target is a useful way to evaluate how well an organisation is operating against its strategy.

Let's consider how we will calculate the KPI '% Bookings Made By Previous Customers'. In our dataset, this is an included column: [is_repeated_guest], so the data we need is readily available. Were this not the case, we would have needed to be able to identify the guest from the booking data and build a lookup table that presented whether or not the guest had booked in a given time period. In this dataset, the guest is anonymous, so the inclusion of [is_repeated_guest] is essential.

Consider the following pseudocode:

% Bookings Made By Previous Guest = Number Of Bookings Where [is_repeated_guest] is True / (Divided By) Number Of Bookings.

This would tell us the proportion of Bookings for which the booking guest is a repeat customer. Let's try it over the whole dataset:

- Open your "Analyse" tab in hotel_bookings.xlsx.
- Under the Booking Volumes By Month analysis, create a new heading, "Repeat Bookings Analysis", and subtitle, "Operations Director".
- Create a grid with the row headings and column headings as follows:

	A	B	C	D	E
33	**Repeat Bookings Analysis**				
34	*Operations Director*				
35		**Total**	**2015**	**2016**	**2017**
36	% Bookings Made By Previous Customers				
37	*No. Bookings Made By Previous Customers*				
38	*No. Bookings*				
39					

- Apply an indent to the row headings in A37 and A38 and italicise the contents of rows 37 and 38. This formatting and inclusion of the component parts of the calculation (the numerator—No. Bookings Made By

Previous Customers; the denominator—No. Bookings) usefully provides the context for the calculated KPI.

- In cell B37, add the formula:

=COUNTIFS(hotel_bookings!$B:$B,0,hotel_bookings!$S:$S,1).

- This counts the number of completed bookings for which [is_repeated_guest] = 1.
- In cell B38, add the formula:

=COUNTIFS(hotel_bookings!$B:$B,0).

- This counts the number of completed bookings.
- In cell B36, add the formula:

=B37/B38.

- Format this cell as a percentage with 1 decimal place. There is a quick button to apply percentage formatting within the Number group on the Home ribbon, or you can use the formatting menu.
- For Total, you should have "4.3%", which is the product of 3,258 bookings from repeat customers of a total of 75,166 bookings.

The KPI calculation is complete for the Operations Director. In the challenge, you will complete the grid to provide these values by year.

Exercise 10 – Challenge

Build upon your knowledge of COUNTIFS() and cell references to calculate the KPI, numerator, and denominator for years 2015, 2016 and 2017 to complete the grid. For an extra challenge, replace the formula in the KPI row (numerator/denominator) with a complete formula that doesn't reference the rows beneath. You won't always have the space or need to provide the component parts to the calculation, so you need to be able to calculate a KPI in a single formula.

When complete, you should have the following:

	A	B	C	D	E
33	Repeat Bookings Analysis				
34	*Operations Director*				
35		**Total**	**2015**	**2016**	**2017**
36	% Bookings Made By Previous Customers	4.3%	2.1%	4.5%	5.3%
37	*No. Bookings Made By Previous Customers*	*3,258*	*289*	*1,643*	*1,326*
38	*No. Bookings*	*75,166*	*13,854*	*36,370*	*24,942*
39					

Exercise 10 – Review

Producing and monitoring KPIs such as this simple example can be a key part of the data analyst role within an organisation, as is understanding and describing why and how KPIs are moving in one direction or another. Sometimes this is about understanding the broader business context (e.g., new hotel—will take some time to develop a pool of regular repeat customers; international pandemic—fewer visitors, particularly older guests) or particular initiatives the hotel is trying in order to influence performance (e.g., customer loyalty programme, developing links with key customers that use hotel for business trips and offering discounts—both of which would have associated data points). At other times, performance cannot be explained in terms that are immediately obvious, and so a deeper analysis project is required to understand performance.

EXERCISE 11

"The Sales & Marketing Director would like to know which market segments produce the most bookings".

In this exercise, we will introduce and learn about one of the most powerful analytical tools in Excel, the PivotTable. We will create a PivotTable, understand its relationship with the data on which it is based and alter some calculations and formatting. You will also appreciate the ease with which some of the earlier exercises could have been completed! Nonetheless, it is important to know how to produce the formulas we have created, as a PivotTable isn't always the solution—particularly when you want more control over the layout.

- When creating a PivotTable, you can either create the PivotTable first and then select the data on which it is based or select the data and then create the PivotTable. Let's try the latter method.
- Create a new worksheet in your workbook and rename it "Market Segment".
- Return to the hotel_bookings sheet and highlight columns A–AM (all the data). With all the data selected, press the PivotTable button on the Insert ribbon:

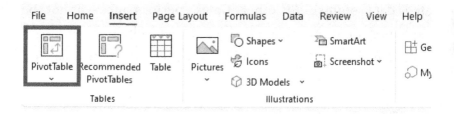

- When the 'PivotTable from table or range' box appears, select "Existing Worksheet" and use the small button on the right-hand side to manually select a destination for your table. Click into the Market Segment worksheet and select cell A1 to auto populate the destination box.

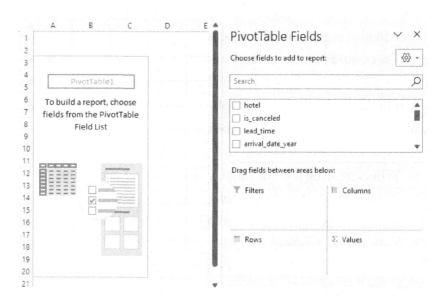

As we can see from the image above, the PivotTable introduces a number of new user interface elements. In the main area of the screen, we have an area designated for the table itself. On the right-hand side, we have the PivotTable Fields pane. Included here are all the columns from our data selection when we made the PivotTable. Had we not selected the entire columns but a subset of the total number of rows, the PivotTable would only consider the rows included. This is possible by accident, so it's worth being aware of this when making a table. However, the range of cells considered by the PivotTable CAN be updated after its creation, which is useful.

When the PivotTable is selected, it also introduces two new menus to the ribbon, PivotTable Analyze ("Options" in older versions of Excel) and Design.

Let's learn the basics by returning to the exercise.

- Click on the empty checkbox next to [is_canceled] in the field list.
- The default behaviour of Excel is to add the selected data to the PivotTable into "Values" and as a "Sum". This is because [is_canceled] is numeric data, and Excel assumes we want to aggregate it in some way—Sum is the default aggregation.
- Let's add another column to our PivotTable. Click on the checkbox next to [market_segment].
- The default behaviour this time is to add this column to the "Rows" part of the PivotTable. This is because the underlying data is Text (name of market segment), and so can't be "added up" in the way our numeric data could. It is treated as "categorical" and so is considered as a *way to segment* the SUM of [is_canceled]. You can see immediately that some market segments contain more records than others— and how quickly you were able to produce this

summary—no formula typing, cell references, and copying.

- The Value "Sum of is_canceled", which Excel has calculated for us, isn't particularly useful to us. It is the number of cancelled bookings by segment—we want the total number of complete bookings for this analysis. Click on "Sum of is_cancelled" in the bottom right grid and drag it to the top left area of the grid, "Filters" ("Report Filter" in older versions of Excel).

- Note how the PivotTable has changed. There are no Values being displayed—we removed the calculation— and there is now a small filter added above the table itself, showing "is_canceled (All)". We are now using the column [is_canceled] as an interactive filter on the table. Click on the filter drop down and notice you can select either of the values for this column (0 or 1). This will allow us to immediately update all the calculations in the table for cancelled, completed or all bookings at the touch of a button. Let's create a new measure, then revisit this.

- We want to create a count of bookings as a Value. As when we used the COUNT() function in an earlier exercise, in a PivotTable we can use any column as all we are doing is counting the number of rows—we are not interested in the specific data in the cells of the column. Like the earlier exercise, however, we must consider only columns with data in every row. The Count function within the PivotTable will not count blank cells. Drag [hotel] from the field list into Values.

- Note this time, the default behaviour of Excel is to create "Count of hotel" as the measure. It cannot create "Sum of hotel" as [hotel] is a text column, so there are no numbers to add up. Check across to the PivotTable. It now contains values again. Note the Grand Total and check the number against your Total Bookings count in an earlier exercise. It should be the same number: 119,390. If it is fewer than this, check that you have no filters applied on [is_canceled] and that your PivotTable is based upon the entire dataset. You can check this by pressing the "Change Data Source" button on the Data Group in the PivotTable Analyze ribbon. Your PivotTable must be selected for this to appear! The Data Source should be set as follows:

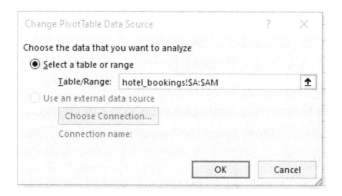

- To demonstrate the flexibility of PivotTables, drag [is_canceled] from Filters to Columns ("Column Labels" in older versions of Excel) in the PivotTable Fields pane. You now have a breakdown of all bookings by market segment, showing completed and cancelled bookings and the total. No formula written!

- Note that the column headers and row headers include "(blank)". This is because we selected the entire columns as our data source and have no filters applied to our table, so as things stand, it thinks we want the empty rows included in the analysis. Use one or both of the Row Labels and Column Labels drop-down buttons to apply a filter to the data. So long as one of your selections does not include "(blank)", the associated columns and rows will disappear from the table
- Return [is_canceled] to the Filters area of the grid and use the drop-down button to apply a filter so that only completed bookings are included (0 only).
- Click on the down arrow next to "Count of hotel" in the Values pane to customise the calculation. Click Value Field Settings . . .
- Give the calculation a new name, "Number of Bookings". Click Number Format and apply "Number", a 1000 separator and 0 decimal places.
- Note that on this settings screen, you can change a calculation from Count to Sum, Average, Min, Max, and more.
- Right-click on a data entry in Number of Bookings column in the PivotTable and click Sort in the context menu which appears and choose "Sort Largest To Smallest" to reorder the data.
- We now have a summary of completed bookings data by market segment, which we could share with the Sales & Marketing Director. Let's take it one step further and improve the summary with an extra column.

- Drag another copy of [hotel] into Values and note that the existing measure is unaffected. Alter the settings for this new entry, renaming it "% of Total Bookings". Then click "Show Values As" to alter the way the data is summarised.

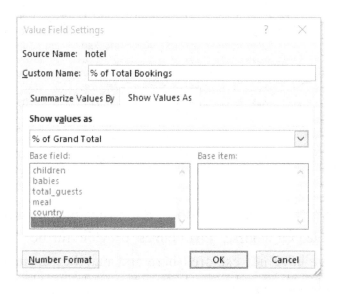

- Select "% of Grand Total" from the drop down, enter Number Format and set the calculation as a Percentage with 1 decimal place, and press OK to confirm changes.
- Look at the resulting table. Note that the inclusion of "% of Total Bookings" helps immediately understand the proportion of bookings represented by the totals. "TA" stands for Travel Agents, and "TO" stands for Tour Operators.
- As a final step, drag [arrival_date_year] into the Columns area of the grid in the Fields pane. Whether you place this above or below the entry for "Values"

changes the layout of the table—try both. Which do you think is the better layout for understanding the by-year values for both Number of Bookings and % of Total Bookings?

Row Labels	Number of Bookings			% of Total Bookings			Total Number of Bookings	Total % of Total Bookings
	2015	2016	2017	2015	2016	2017		
Online TA	4,520	17,824	13,394	6.0%	23.7%	17.8%	35,738	47.5%
Offline TA/TO	4,012	8,143	3,753	5.3%	10.8%	5.0%	15,908	21.2%
Direct	1,963	4,796	3,913	2.6%	6.4%	5.2%	10,672	14.2%
Groups	2,257	3,005	2,452	3.0%	4.0%	3.3%	7,714	10.3%
Corporate	952	2,187	1,164	1.3%	2.9%	1.5%	4,303	5.7%
Complementary	150	317	179	0.2%	0.4%	0.2%	646	0.9%
Aviation		98	87	0.0%	0.1%	0.1%	185	0.2%
Grand Total	13,854	36,370	24,942	18.4%	48.4%	33.2%	75,166	100.0%

With that, we have understood the basic functionality of a PivotTable. Of course, PivotTables provide further features which we have not explored here and may be the subject of another book in future.

Exercise 11 – Challenge

This challenge contains two parts. Firstly, consider the % values in the table. Note that the annual breakdown we included contains figures which add up to the Grand Total—this is how we originally set up "% of Total Bookings". Revisit this step and try some of the other calculation options under "Show Values As". Find the setting that will express the percentages in such a way that they add up to 100% for each year rather than across the total.

The second part of this exercise's challenge is optional but will quickly familiarise you with all the features we just explored. Revisit the exercises in this chapter and recreate the analyses using a PivotTable. You need not worry about recreating the same output layout, but summarising the data in the same way is possible. Try it now—you'll be much more familiar with the set up and creation of new tables, adding calculations and changing their labelling and format.

Exercise 11 – Review

In this exercise, we learned about PivotTables and their value in quickly summarising information. Given the speed with which you can quickly summarise data, they are very useful for exploring a dataset and trying to make sense of it before building something more formal, like a report or dashboard, which requires a specific layout.

We produced an analysis of market segment for the Director, which showed the contribution of each segment to each year's total and the same for the entire dataset. If the data contained booking records for multiple full years, it would make sense to go further and interpret the data—perhaps to describe the growth of one segment year on year and its growing importance to the business. However, both 2015 and 2017 are partial years, so they are not representative of a full year of operations. It is also the case that in an organisation, you might be involved in the creation and data capture of a new business process (e.g., creation of a new market segment) but are months or years away from being able to meaningfully analyse it, as the data has never been gathered before!

EXERCISE 12

"The Sales & Marketing Director wants to present a new strategy on room pricing to his team and would like a chart which shows that the price charged per room per night is lower the further in advance the customer books".

In this exercise, we will need to learn how to produce a chart for the first time to visualise our data and satisfy the Director's request. Note that the Director is confident about the relationship between how far in advance a room is booked and the price charged. In this instance, we are investigating their hypothesis rather than one of our own. Aren't all the best deals found last minute? Let's find out.

Let's first consider what the chart will need to show. We have thousands of data points for Average Daily Rate [adr] and [lead_time] and for any given lead time, presumably, multiple bookings and rates charged. Do we want to show all of them? The value of a chart is to visually show the *relationship* between two more or more pieces of data (e.g., sales and time, or bookings and customer segment, etc.). We don't need to see every piece of information we have to draw out a relationship—just values representing it. In this case, we can take all of our lead time data and present the *average* room rate charged for that lead time. The average still represents the rate charged for a given lead time without needing to display every data point we have. To do this, we need to summarise our data for the chart.

- Create a new worksheet in our workbook and rename it "Lead Time Analysis".
- We need to take a copy of all our lead time data and paste it into this new sheet. Select column C in the hotel_bookings sheet, copy it and paste it into cell A1 in Lead Time Analysis.
- We will have multiple entries for each lead time value— select the whole column and click Sort & Filter in the Editing group on the Home ribbon. Click Sort Smallest To Largest and note how many 0s appear at the top of the list!
- We want to condense this data down to a list of unique values—we only need to calculate the average ADR for each lead time once. With the whole column selected, click on the "Data" ribbon and find the "Remove Duplicates" button:

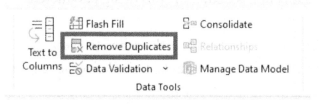

- On the following screen, leave "My data has headers" selected and ensure the column "lead_time" is selected in the bottom pane. Press OK.
- A box will appear announcing this has completed. Most of the values will be removed, leaving over 400 unique entries. You should now have a list that starts like this:

	A	B
1	lead_time	
2	0	
3	1	
4	2	
5	3	
6	4	

- In cell B1, add the column name "Average_ADR" and in cell B2, add the following formula:

=AVERAGEIFS(hotel_bookings!AD:AD,hotel_bookings!C:C,'Lead Time Analysis'!A2).

- This formula is taking the following parameters:

  ○ The [adr] column (AD) as the range to average.
  ○ The [lead_time] column (C) to look for the specific lead time value for which to calculate an average.
  ○ The actual lead time—for row 2, we are considering the lead time value '0' that is in A2—the cell next to it.
  ○ In other words, average the values in AD if C contains a 0.

- Copy the formula down to the bottom so that every value in column A has a value in column B. Format

Average_ADR so that it is a Number with 0 decimal places. You should have something like this:

	A	B
1	lead_time	Average_ADR
2	0	83
3	1	90
4	2	94
5	3	93
6	4	95

- We have the data we need! Let's make a chart. As with PivotTables, you can start by selecting some data and then inserting a Chart, or you can create a Chart and then select the data. We'll do the latter.
- Click into a blank cell to the right of the data and click on the Insert ribbon. Find the Charts group and click on the Line Chart icon as shown:

- Select the simple Line Chart option on the top left of the window which appears. A white box with no detail will appear in your spreadsheet—this is our Chart—we just need to add some data.
- Two new ribbon menus will appear if the chart is selected — "Chart Design" and "Format". With Chart

Design selected, find the "Select Data" button in the
Data group and press it.

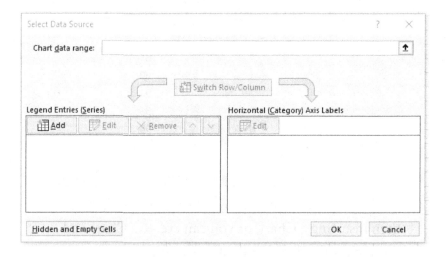

- There are two options here: one can either select an
  entire data range, and Excel will interpret it and create
  some series to chart (a "series" is the line which will
  appear and represents a column of data visually), or we
  can create our series manually. Let's do this.
- Press the Add button. In the box which appears, give
  the series the name "Average Rate", and for the second
  option, use the Up Arrow button to manually select
  your data:

- Click into cell B2, the first entry under Average_ADR, on your Lead Time Analysis sheet and press CTRL+SHIFT+Down Arrow to select every entry in the column. Note that if you include the column title, it will try to plot the text alongside the numbers and will fail! Hit Return or press the button in the control box to submit the cell range.
- Next, we need to declare the values for the x-axis— "Horizontal (Category) Axis Labels"—the values along the bottom of the chart. Press the Edit button in the right-hand pane of Select Data Source and repeat the process above, only for the values in column A, beginning in cell A2.
- Press OK to confirm the chart and view the results:

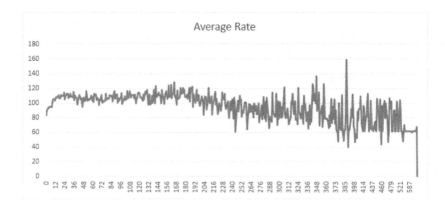

What do you notice about the direction of the line chart? It appears as though the general trend is downward between ADR (Y Axis/Vertical Axis) and Lead Time (X Axis/Horizontal Axis), so the chart does appear to be showing the relationship between the two variables that the Sales & Marketing Director suggested. It also appears that the 'common sense' view that you can get good deals at short notice also applies—look at the relationship between ADR and Lead Time if the booking is made within 30 days of arrival. It appears to go up from around 80 to 110 before stabilising and entering the gentle downward relationship with Lead Time that was hypothesised. Let's make the chart a little easier to read and apply some extra formatting.

- First, let's try one of the pre-selected Chart Styles that are available. Make sure the chart is selected, and hover your mouse to the right-hand side of it. You may need to click on the chart a second time. Three small buttons should appear: a Plus for adding chart elements, a Paintbrush for applying styles, and a Funnel for applying filters. All of these options are also in the ribbon if this doesn't appear. Use the Paintbrush and scroll through some of the pre-selected Styles and choose one you like. Broadly, any selection here should enhance the readability of the data—that is your primary concern. Consistent "branding" across a report is also useful, except where it oversimplifies or makes a chart harder to read. These style options also appear in the "Chart Design" ribbon when the chart is selected.

- Use the Plus button or Add Chart Element button on the Chart Design ribbon and add an "Axis Title" for the "Primary Horizontal" axis (x axis). When "Axis Title" text is added to your chart, edit it and rename the axis "Lead Time (Days")".

- In the same way, add a "Primary Vertical" axis title and rename it "Average Daily Rate".

- Edit the chart title (currently "Average Rate") to "Average Daily Rate vs Lead Time".

- Use Add Chart Element to add a Trendline and select "Linear". This creates a simple "line of best fit" to the data and can help to simplify a relationship visually. Carefully select the trendline, right-click on it and press "Format Trendline", and this should open the formatting pane. This applies to any chart element— click and format to customise it. Give the trendline a suitable colour and style so that it is visually distinct from the data itself.

Our chart is now easier to read, the relationship between the two variables is clearer with the trendline, and the axes have titles, so it's obvious to someone looking at the chart for the first time what the data is describing.

When presenting this chart in a business setting, you would likely include some commentary alongside, highlighting the main observations produced by the analysis. Namely, that there is an inverse relationship between Lead Time and ADR (as Lead Time increases, ADR achieved falls)—except in the short term (under 30 days) wherein the opposite is true (the more "last minute" your booking, the better the deal you can get).

Exercise 12 – Challenge

In this challenge, we will make the chart even easier to read by addressing the "noise" in the chart—that is to say, the line oscillates wildly around the trend with sharp peaks and troughs. We can make the line smoother by summarising the data further. At present, we have included every unique value for Lead Time and presented the Average of ADR achieved for bookings with that Lead Time. Now, we will summarise Lead Time and present the data in 5-day buckets: i.e., Bookings made with a Lead Time of 0–5 days, 6–10 days, 11–15 days, etc. For this, we return to "Prepare" and reconfigure our data to enable a new analysis.

- Create a new column in hotel_bookings and give it a column heading "lead_time_bucket" (column AN).
- In AN2, type the formula:

=ROUNDUP(C2/5,0)*5.

- This takes the value in C2 (the lead_time for that booking), divides it by 5, rounds up the answer, and multiples this by 5 again to determine the closest multiple of 5 buckets that the actual lead time would sit in. Here's an example:
- Lead Time = 41. Divide by 5 = 8.2. Round up to 9. Multiply by 5 = 45. So "41" is in the 40–45 Lead Time Bucket (presented as "45" on the chart).
- Copy the formula down and rebuild your chart using this new column instead of lead_time. You will need to repeat the "Average ADR" step of preparing the data and removing duplicates from the Lead Time Bucket.

Good luck! Do you think the new chart is an improvement?

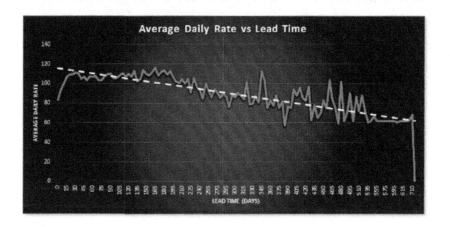

Exercise 12 – Review

In this exercise, we produced a line chart and explored some basic customisation options. There are many types of charts, and each is better suited to some applications over others. In some cases, this is obvious. In other cases, there isn't a clear choice, and how you present your analysis becomes a matter of personal choice. A whole book could be written on the visual presentation of data, so the purpose of this exercise was merely to introduce you to the production of a chart in Excel.

We also looked at reducing noise in the data by further summarising it using lead_time_bucket instead of lead_time. Arguably, both charts visualise the *relationship* equally well. The bucket version perhaps makes reading off a value from the chart easier. For example, using the bucket version allows you to infer that the peak ADR is achieved at around a lead time of 165 days—what would you do with that information? Well, it might be that you can achieve the best profit on a room booking by advertising to potential customers for a trip they might take in around 6 months' time. A potential summer vacation marketed in the depths of winter, perhaps? This is a practical example of using data analysis to inform strategy to have a real-world impact (increase profitability). By contrast, the unbucketed data shows a peak value at around 390 days' lead time. This makes less sense when you consider the downward relationship between ADR and Lead Time, and with summarisation, the peak disappears and is revealed as an anomaly.

CHAPTER SUMMARY/KEY TAKEAWAYS

We covered a lot in this chapter, as you might expect. We looked at:

- Aggregate functions (e.g., SUM, COUNT, AVERAGE, MIN, MAX) and their value in exploring and describing datasets.
- The COUNT(), SUM(), COUNTIF() and SUMIF() functions in practice—both to answer the Director's requests and also to go a step beyond and provide a more valuable, contextualised analysis.
- The importance of checking your output by way of comparing subtotals and totals.
- Responding to incomplete data (3 years' data in the dataset, of which 2 years were incomplete) with responsive formulas and the provision of underlying data for context.
- Completing summary outputs using both dynamic and fixed cell references.

- AVERAGE() and AVERAGEIF() functions with the business application for the use of averages.
- Conditional formatting.
- Developing a Key Performance Indicator and how to present performance data.
- PivotTables—their power, flexibility and speed.
- Charting and summarisation techniques to display relationships.

In the next chapter, we will consider some broader business questions which force us to develop some hypotheses of our own and consider how we will develop an impactful analysis that tells a story.

CHAPTER 8
CONSIDER

I n this chapter, the final of the 3-step process, we will examine some broader business questions which are deliberately less focused, putting the responsibility on you, the analyst, to determine which analyses best answer the question. Thus, you must consider what is relevant and impactful.

It is not enough to crunch the numbers and hope someone else can make sense of it. The analyst creates a story with their work, and like any good story, it must be interesting and tailored to the audience. Let us quickly revisit some of the key elements of Consider that we discussed in Chapter 4.

- Producing an output which addresses the *problem statement* in a manner *suited to the audience.*
- This is about creating an *impactful message* using analyses that *have value and are relevant to the problem.*

- Understanding your audience includes considering *seniority, ability to influence, intended use of the information, data literacy, area of interest,* and *the recipient's personal tastes.*
- Awareness (again) of the *limitations of the data.* How confident are you in your recommendations—would you act upon them?

With that, let's look at some new concepts that support this aim.

CONTEXTUAL DATA

When presenting information, or indeed when reviewing information and trying to form a decision, it is important to understand the broader context. It is not always enough to measure the performance of one's own organisation. If the hotel increases its bookings this year by 5%—is that good? It would be quite an achievement during a global pandemic but less impressive in a year when the sector itself grows by 10%—a loss of market share. When producing an output, the use of contextual data should support the reader in understanding the significance of your calculations. If the question *"so what?"* could occur to your audience, you have not produced an analysis that fully supports them in executing their role.

Typically in an organisational context, analysis of performance should be supported by comparison to any targets the business has set itself and any data from the wider sector that allows you to understand your performance in relation to others.

However, this information is not always readily available, so this is not true for many situations. You should nevertheless try to seek information which contextualises your analysis wherever possible. Information which allows you to compare yourself directly to your competitors can be impossible to source as it is commercially valuable to hide your operational performance from your competitors. One example of publicly available competitor information is published accounts, but this only covers financial information. An organisation will otherwise strongly protect its data on its customers, products, and operations.

An organisation which is effective in its setting of targets will often take into consideration both internal and external factors when deciding where it wishes to grow or improve and by how much. This process can include an analysis of the health of the industry, the effectiveness of competitors, the political and economic environment and internal factors such as organisational strategy. For example, focussing on improving customer satisfaction instead of growth of bookings or acquiring new premises this year so as to improve its brand image before seeking to expand. Where this process has been undertaken effectively, measuring performance against target can be a suitable compromise if contextual information from the industry is unavailable. The organisation's strategy already reflects an analysis of these external forces and has been adjusted accordingly.

INFORMATION VS INSIGHT

In the world of data analytics and business intelligence, much is made of the word "insight"—what does it mean? You may have seen an image like this before:

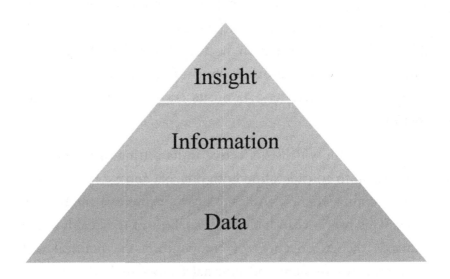

- Data is a collection of observations and labels which are too numerous in an unprocessed form to be interpreted.
- Information is the expression of the pattern or summarised value of the Data.
- Insight is the interpretation of the Information that can be acted upon.

One of the more common mistakes made by analysts in their role is to produce Information from Data and simply present this information to the audience so that they can form their own Insights. To be clear, sometimes this *is* all you are asked to do: your audience may prefer to come to their own Insights, be data literate, and have an excellent level of domain knowledge to apply to their interpretation. However, problems arise when your audience does not have this appetite for information, but that is all they are given.

Insight is rarely created by the perfect analysis of a single piece of information. Rather, it takes an information set and combines it into a conclusion of high value. The outputs we produced in Analyse have broadly taken Data and turned it into Information. In each of the fictional scenarios containing a request from a Director, Information was requested. However, when we come to the exercises in this chapter, our directors will be looking for Insight, and so we will need to perform multiple analyses of data to create an Information set from which to determine and recommend a course of action: Insight.

EXERCISE 13

In this exercise, we will consider a much more open-ended request from management that will see us undertake a variety of analyses and present back an output which brings together an insightful answer from which action can be taken.

"The Sales & Marketing Director is considering a new customer acquisition strategy for 2018, focussing on improving profitability across both hotel sites. Investigate our bookings data from 2015-2017 and support the director with any valuable insights from the dataset".

Requests of this nature are common in data analysis, though how frequently you will be given work of this nature can vary by role. Note that we have not been given any hypotheses to explore—we will have to come up with our own, analyse them, and *consider* their value and relevance in the development of a customer acquisition strategy.

What are the objectives of an effective customer acquisition strategy with profitability as a specific focus? All businesses seek to maximise profit, and a hotel with a fixed room capacity can achieve this by *achieving the highest price per room that it can* and *by utilising all of its available capacity* (assuming that all the staff required to operate the hotel will be employed either way). Such a strategy may also have other **objectives**:

1. **Market share**: A strategy may be designed to increase the hotel chain's market share by setting prices lower than competitors. This approach can help the hotel chain attract price-sensitive customers who might otherwise choose a competitor.
2. **Brand image**: A strategy may be designed to reinforce the hotel chain's brand image by setting prices at a premium level or by deliberately appealing to particular customer groups. This approach can help the hotel chain establish a reputation for luxury and exclusivity or for being family-friendly.
3. **Customer loyalty**: A strategy may be designed to encourage customer loyalty by offering discounts or other incentives to customers who book directly with the hotel. This approach can help the hotel chain build a base of loyal customers who return for future stays.

4. **Occupancy rate**: A strategy may be designed to maintain a high occupancy rate by setting prices lower during periods of low demand. This approach can help the hotel chain maintain a steady flow of revenue, even during slow periods.

5. **Revenue diversification**: A strategy may be designed to diversify revenue streams by offering additional services or amenities at a price. This approach can help the hotel chain generate revenue from sources other than room bookings.

For a given set of objectives, what **methods** might an organisation deploy to develop an effective customer acquisition strategy for increasing profitability?

1. **Customer segmentation**: The hotel chain can segment its customers based on demographics, travel purpose, length of stay, and other relevant factors. By doing so, the hotel chain can offer differentiated pricing to each customer segment. For example, business travellers may be willing to pay higher rates than leisure travellers, and guests who book in advance may be offered a discount.

2. **Dynamic pricing**: The hotel chain can use dynamic pricing to adjust room rates based on demand, supply, and other market conditions. Dynamic pricing can help the hotel chain optimize revenue by offering discounts during low-demand periods and increasing prices during high-demand periods.

3. **Revenue management**: The hotel chain can use revenue management techniques to forecast demand, optimize inventory, and set prices. Revenue management can help the hotel chain allocate rooms to the right customers at the right time and at the right price.

4. **Competitive pricing**: The hotel chain can monitor the prices of its competitors and adjust its own prices accordingly. This can help the hotel chain stay competitive while also maximizing revenue.

5. **Loyalty programs**: The hotel chain can offer loyalty programs to reward customers who book directly with the hotel. Loyalty programs can incentivize customers to book directly with the hotel, which can reduce commissions paid to online travel agencies and increase revenue for the hotel chain.

6. **Seasonal pricing**: The hotel chain can adjust its room rates based on seasonal demand. For example, rates may be higher during peak tourist season and lower during off-peak season.

7. **Package pricing**: The hotel chain can offer package pricing that includes room, meals, and other services. Package pricing can help the hotel chain increase revenue by bundling multiple services together and offering them at a discounted price.

A working knowledge of both the **objectives** of an organisation in a given industry and the associated **methods** one could use to achieve this are examples of Domain Knowledge. Experience in developing solutions using a method to achieve an objective is what potential employers seek and value highly. A track record in delivering analysis and insight to support this work is a stronger testament to your potential value to an organisation than a set of technical skills alone.

Let's return to our data and the request of the director. Profit is the difference between Revenue (the money received for selling goods or services) and Cost (the money paid out to staff, suppliers, creditors, and so on to enable those goods or services to be delivered). In the case of the hotel, here are some specific aspects to consider:

- Our Revenue is our [booking_revenue]—the ADR multiplied by the number of nights stayed.
- The ADR achieved may vary by the [customer_type], their [board_basis], their booking [lead_time], where they booked from ([country_name]), [reserved_room_type], [market_segment], [distribution_channel], party composition ([adults], [children], and [babies]), the time of year ([arrival_date_month]), and so on
- Repeat customers may book directly with the hotel, avoiding 3rd party commissions, and so incur a lower 'cost of acquisition'.[1]
- Bookings which include meals incur a higher cost to the hotel (providing food), but the associated ADR increase *may* mean more profit is made on the booking.
- Many costs are fixed (e.g., repayments on loans for the purchase of the hotel, energy, maintenance, and essential staff) for the purposes of the strategy.

- The Resort Hotel and City Hotel may have a different customer or booking profile so are worth considering separately.

How do we begin to analyse the data? We have explored a number of hypotheses above—namely that *some of the customer characteristics will be associated with higher profit per booking*. If we investigate ADR and how it varies from group to group, we can start to understand *which types of customers we want to attract*. We don't have a set of full information, including operational running costs, but we know from our historical booking data *what price different groups will pay* for the same experience.

Let's make a start on the analyses. From now on, the exercises offer less specific instructions, so be ready to spend a little more time thinking through your approach:

- Create a new worksheet in the hotel_bookings workbook. Give it a meaningful name. You may need to create several over the course of this exercise.
- Create a pivot table based on the hotel_bookings dataset (repeating the instructions on page 79) and explore the relationship between average [adr] and some of the columns mentioned above ([customer_type], [board_basis], and so on) for each hotel. Wherever you find a significant difference in ADR between one group and another, take a copy of the worksheet or copy the data in the PivotTable range to another sheet to build up a series of analyses that may be useful later.

- Try combining columns in your PivotTable to drill down into the details. For example, how does ADR vary by Arrival Month for each Distribution Channel? How does this vary by hotel?
- It can be useful to summarise in words the findings from each analysis so that you don't have to reinterpret your saved work each time you look at it. Here's an example:

Row Labels	January	February	March	April	May	June	July	August	September	October	November	December	Grand Total
is_canceled	0	.T											
Average of adr	Columr												
City Hotel	82.2	86.2	90.2	111.9	120.4	117.7	115.6	118.4	112.6	101.7	86.5	87.9	105.7
Corporate	68.1	69.6	79.3	88.2	95.7	96.8	81.8	71.3	95.9	81.9	74.4	68.8	82.8
Direct	83.6	89.4	90.7	118.7	130.0	120.7	121.5	123.1	120.7	112.7	85.3	93.1	110.4
GDS	88.7	93.9	94.9	94.4	152.5	136.1	156.8	151.0	179.4	112.4	132.8	84.6	119.9
TA/TO	83.4	86.6	90.8	111.9	121.3	119.0	116.1	119.1	112.6	101.9	88.2	88.6	106.6
Resort Hotel	48.7	54.1	57.0	75.9	76.7	107.9	150.1	181.2	96.4	61.7	48.7	68.3	90.8
Corporate	36.8	42.1	42.3	53.7	51.0	71.7	126.5	137.4	82.1	54.7	38.1	34.2	51.5
Direct	51.3	59.0	63.5	85.6	87.4	128.5	164.1	202.4	115.9	65.1	56.8	94.8	102.3
TA/TO	49.4	54.4	57.7	75.8	76.0	104.4	146.6	175.4	92.3	63.2	49.6	61.7	92.1
Undefined								112.7					112.7
Grand Total	67.0	72.4	77.3	97.9	104.8	114.6	129.3	142.1	107.3	86.8	70.5	78.9	100.0

Notes

City
Rates are less seasonal than Resort. Direct bookings and the GDS channel achieve the best ADR. Average Rates over >100 are achievable between Apr - Oct

Resort
Highly seasonal. Best rates achieved in July and August - summer vacation time in Europe. Direct bookings achieve the best ADR, followed by Travel Agents and Tour Operators

- It will also be required at times to check the validity of some of your observations. Here's a pivot of [board_basis] and [distribution_channel] showing the Average ADR and a Count of Bookings:

is_canceled	0									
	Corporate		Direct		GDS		TA/TO		Undefined	
Row Labels	Av. ADR	Bookings	Av. ADR	Bookings	Av. ADR	Bookings	Av. ADR	Bookings	Av. ADR	Bookings
City Hotel	82.8	2,622	110.4	5,548	119.9	156	106.6	37,902		
Bed & Breakfast	82.7	2,592	108.3	5,009	124.9	94	107.2	27,943		
Full Board			26.9	8			206.0	1		
Half Board	120.4	16	170.8	221			116.2	3,743		
No Meal Package	53.9	14	103.0	310	112.3	62	98.3	6,215		
Resort Hotel	51.5	2,581	102.3	6,540			92.1	19,816	112.7	1
Bed & Breakfast	50.0	2,401	92.0	5,109			86.1	14,652		
Full Board	99.0	14	155.4	106			127.6	191		
Half Board	67.8	113	145.7	1,069			112.7	4,316	112.7	1
No Meal Package	70.9	53	105.0	256			79.5	657		
Grand Total	67.2	5,203	106.0	12,088	119.9	156	101.6	57,718	112.7	1

Notes
City
Best rates are achieved on Half Board Direct Bookings. Full Board does not appear to be a standard option based on no. bookings, so can be discarded
Resort
Full and Half Board Direct Bookings achieve the best ADR. There is not a big difference in rates and Full Board is taken by relatively few guests so it may not be worth continuing the service

- Note that the data on Full Board bookings at the City Hotel is based on so few bookings that they are likely exceptions, and this board basis is not routinely offered and so shouldn't feature in the strategy.

- It was also observed that for the Resort Hotel, Full Board does not attract a significantly higher rate than Half Board, and relatively few guests book Full Board, so there may be an operational saving in no longer offering a lunch service. Whilst this is outside the scope of *customer acquisition*, these observations can be very valuable and should be shared. One of the most satisfying aspects of data analysis work is discovering highly valuable insight before anyone else!

- Here's a pivot of [total_guests] (party size 0 removed) and [customer_type]:

is_canceled	0	.T					
Av. ADR	**Total Guest .T**						
Hotel	**1**	**2**	**3**	**4**	**5**	**10**	**12**
City Hotel	90.0	102.2	140.6	190.5	243.3	95.0	84.5
Contract	108.7	104.5	125.1	163.5	153.0		
Group	86.4	84.3	113.6	134.7	270.0		
Transient	92.6	104.6	142.7	192.9	246.8		84.5
Transient-Party	85.6	95.9	124.4	177.7	188.4	95.0	
Resort Hotel	52.9	91.6	140.3	175.6	169.4		
Contract	53.7	78.5	107.4	130.1			
Group	50.4	85.4	144.2	137.4			
Transient	52.7	95.6	146.5	178.0	169.4		
Transient-Party	53.5	82.6	118.1	150.4			
Grand Total	**76.5**	**98.0**	**140.5**	**183.1**	**218.9**	**95.0**	**84.5**

Notes
City
Group and transient bookings attract the best rates with larger booking parties associated with higher ADR. Note that there may be few rooms that can accommodate larger groups.
Resort
Group and transient bookings attract the best rates with larger booking parties associated with higher ADR. Solo travellers attract a particularly poor ADR

- In both cases, Group (assume multiple rooms booked at the same time for a larger party, e.g., travelling sports team or school trip, etc.) and Transient (not a group or contract booking and no associated bookings)[2] customer types produced the best ADR and the larger the group, the greater the revenue, suggesting pricing is on a per head, not per room basis. For this reason, *increasing the occupancy per room maximises profit*, although any hotel has a fixed supply of any given room type, so there is an upper limit on how far you can push this strategy. Note that solo travellers to the Resort Hotel represent a particularly poor ADR. This is often why solo travellers have to pay a supplemental fee for their room, and this could feature in our recommendations.

- Continue in this manner, developing an understanding of which factors influence an increased ADR by room. Produce 8–10 such analyses, including notes on the observations in each case.

You may now realise that the exploratory stage of an analysis for an open-ended business question can take some time! For this reason, the exercise won't take you through every combination of columns and calculations. We will consider in the next exercise how best to present the information above and package it into a series of recommendations for the Sales & Marketing Director.

Exercise 13 – Challenge

The development of the new customer acquisition strategy reinforces the value of the 3-step model for producing analysis. We began this chapter with a dataset we had started to develop during the "Prepare" chapter and developed further during the "Analyse" chapter. We are now again presented with a scenario where further development of the original dataset could add value.

- Develop at least one new column in hotel_bookings, analyse it, make any observations, and add it to your collection of analyses for consideration.
- If you are stuck for ideas, try developing a descriptive column, [party_type], that looks at the make-up of the guests in the booking and gives it a useful label:

○ "Solo traveller" (1 adult, 0 children, 0 babies)
○ "Couple" (2 adults, 0 children, 0 babies)
○ "Family" (>0 adults, >0 children, 0 babies)
○ "Family with Babies" (>0 adults, >0 babies)
○ Else "Other"

- Perform an analysis of these Party Types and note your observations. How might the output be useful in considering which groups to target with marketing?

Exercise 13 – Review

In this exercise, we began by analysing the request from the Sales & Marketing Director: first, by considering what the key components of a customer acquisition strategy are and second, by looking at some specific mechanisms to improve profit or revenue by booking. This gave us a framework within which to develop some hypotheses to explore: for example, by segmenting customer groups, considering booking lead time, seasonality of demand, and so on.

We explored some of these hypotheses using PivotTables and recorded our observations in relation to the maximisation of Average Daily Rate. These observations will be the basis upon which we develop an output to give back to the director. If you successfully completed the challenge, you also revisited the "Prepare" step to further develop the dataset in relation to the request of the business. Remember that the three steps can be repeated multiple times so long as the problem you are trying to solve is better served by improving the data you have available for analysis.

Our collection of tables and notes does not tell a story on their own, and handed over in their current form, still requires too much of the audience to piece together their own narrative. The next exercise will focus on this.

EXERCISE 14

As suggested above, our collection of analyses and observations, whilst interesting, are not packaged in such a way that the audience can be in no doubt as to how to interpret the results. We are also dealing with a senior audience whose time is limited and so it is our responsibility to develop a story or narrative around our observations which is impactful, insightful, and from which action can be taken.

During Exercise 13, you completed a number of analyses from which useful conclusions could be drawn. We will focus for now on those which were included for demonstration. You will be able to continue on with the additional observations you made using your own PivotTable analyses.

Three analyses were included for demonstration. They were:

1. ADR by month and distribution channel.
2. ADR by board basis and distribution channel.
3. ADR by party size and customer type.

For each of these, we will improve the presentation of the data and include a specific recommendation for the director to consider. We will group the recommendations thematically by **method** (e.g., Customer Segmentation, Dynamic Pricing, etc.)

as these are groupings that the Sales & Marketing Director will be familiar with in their role and may have a preference for one or more of these approaches to developing a strategy. In this way, we recognise the **language of our audience** but give them options so that they may use their experience to decide the best course of action. Remember that we are *supporting the director with [. . .] insight'*.

- For this exercise, we will focus on producing a short written report (e.g., using Microsoft Word or equivalent) for the Sales & Marketing Director. Alternatives to this include producing a slide show (e.g., using Microsoft PowerPoint or equivalent) or an Excel workbook or sheet(s) formatted for printing or exporting to PDF. The slide show output is more appropriate to a shorter update where less or no supporting evidence is required. The Excel workbook is more appropriate when more data is included in the output, and less space is required for explanation. Create a new document in the software of your choice.
- Give the document a suitable heading, such as "Customer Acquisition Strategy Recommendations", and save it with an appropriate file name.
- Create subheadings for the following—they may not all be used and so can be deleted at the end:

   ○ Analysis & Observations
   ○ Customer Segmentation
   ○ Dynamic Pricing
   ○ Revenue Management

○ Competitive Pricing

○ Loyalty Programs

○ Seasonal Pricing

○ Package Pricing

- We will consider our previous analysis of ADR by month and Distribution Channel and produce a series of charts to answer some hypotheses. Once completed, we will write up a recommendation.
- The PivotTable led us to the following observations:

○ The Resort Hotel has more price volatility (bigger difference between highest and lowest ADR achieved) than the City Hotel.

○ Direct Bookings and the GDS ("Global Distribution System")[3] support the best ADR for the City Hotel. Direct and Travel Agent/Tour Operator ADR are the best channels for the Resort Hotel.

○ The Undefined channel for Resort is not regularly used/valid data, so will be excluded from analyses.

- This means the following hypotheses are worth exploring:

○ Some channels are clearly better than others from an ADR perspective but may themselves be seasonal, meaning one outperforms another at a given time of year but not at other periods.

○ There is a period of time during which rates are above average (high season) and below average (low season) for both hotels, and this period may be different for both hotels. This means recommendations focussing on each hotel may apply to different months of the year.

- Let's add some content to **Analysis & Observations**. Produce a line chart containing four series (City Hotel ADR by Month; Resort Hotel ADR by Month; City Annual Average ADR by Month; and Resort Annual Average ADR by Month), adding styling to improve the presentation of the data. Here's an example:

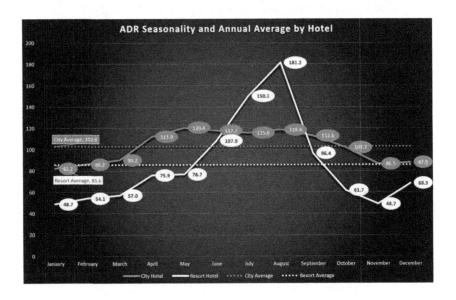

- Tip: To produce an annual average for either hotel, create a formula for January to December which calculates the same AVERAGE() across the fixed range of ADR values for the hotel. This means your formula will create the same value for each month of the year, creating a flat horizontal line. Below this line, ADR is "below average" for the hotel and vice versa.

- Beneath the chart, include the commentary "The chart above clearly demonstrates the volatility and seasonality of both hotels. It also shows the comparative durations of each hotel's "high season". This is April to September for the City Hotel and June to September for the Resort Hotel".

- Produce a column chart that shows annual average ADR by Distribution Channel for each hotel, including the average. This will demonstrate at a glance the extent to which each channel is either above or below average ADR for the hotel. Here's an example:

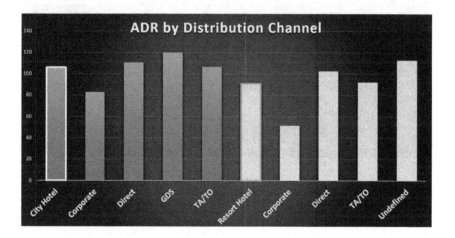

- Take advantage of styling options to colour-code one hotel differently to the other and add a border to the hotel average values to highlight these in comparison to the distribution channel values themselves.

- Include the commentary "We can see clearly that Corporate rates bring down the average for both hotels, but this is particularly true for the Resort Hotel. It is also interesting to note that GDS achieves higher rates than Direct for the City Hotel. We do not know if there is a greater cost in acquiring bookings through this channel though (e.g., commissions or fees)". This chart helps to contextualise any channel-specific recommendations that are not related to seasonality.

- Produce two matching line charts which plot ADR by Distribution Channel and Month for each hotel:

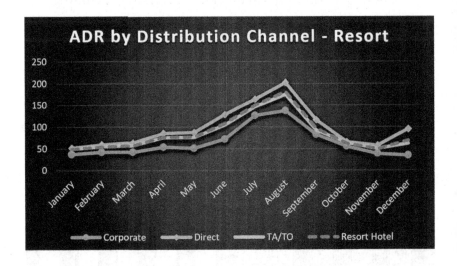

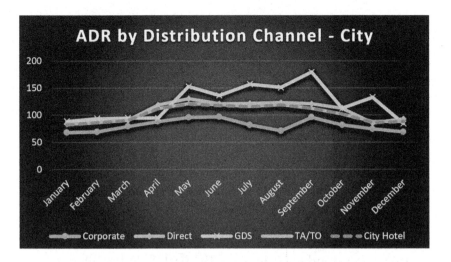

- Include the commentary underneath the first chart, "The Resort Hotel chart shows a clear seasonality for all channels, with Direct bookings producing the best ADR throughout the year".

- Underneath the second, include "The City Hotel chart is more interesting and shows GDS outperforming other channels consistently throughout the year (except April), particularly during high season. Corporate is consistently the source of lowest ADR, and this is particularly true during high season, suggesting a strategy which changes target distribution channel based on month of arrival may be appropriate".

- Let's write up some initial recommendations based on these charts and observations.

- Under "Customer Segmentation", create a bulleted list and an initial recommendation.

○ "Customers booking directly are likely to incur the lowest cost of acquisition and achieve a high ADR for both sites—particularly the Resort Hotel. Further analysis of customer profiles associated with Direct bookings may influence marketing strategy and is required".

○ We include this because a "Direct" booking is not a customer characteristic—it is simply *how* they booked. However, some types of customers (e.g., families with young children) may be more loyal to a particular hotel if they had a good experience in the past. Solo travellers may be more willing to try something new each time and be less loyal. We don't *know* this to be true yet. This is a new hypothesis identified during this analysis.

- Under "Dynamic Pricing", create a bulleted list and an initial recommendation.

○ "ADR achieved by both sites, but particularly the Resort Hotel, is seasonal, and so the room price achievable can vary throughout the year. Annual profitability may depend strongly on taking advantage of higher prices during high seasons, and so, with close attention to competitor pricing, room rates should be held as high as possible during high season. The GDS channel used by the City Hotel achieves the best rates during high season and should be the preferred booking source for the City Hotel at these times of year. This analysis could be improved with use of acquisition cost per channel data".

○ With this comment, we underline the importance of taking advantage of periods of high demand by retaining high prices where possible. A caveat is added to reflect our lack of cost data associated with bookings by each channel, which may undermine the strength of arguing for one over another when considering the profit per booking.

- Under "Competitive Pricing", create a bulleted list and an initial recommendation.

○ "Competitor prices should be monitored throughout the year to ensure that the correct balance is struck between booking volume and ADR. This is particularly true for the Resort Hotel, which could have a poor high season if prices are set too high, booking volumes are low as a result, and profit cannot be recovered during the low season".
○ This is a common sense recommendation that is included so that the recommendation "set prices as high as possible" above isn't taken out of context and potential customers switch to an alternative hotel in the area that offers a better balance of price and comfort/facilities/board/etc.

- Under "Loyalty Programmes", create a bulleted list and an initial recommendation.

○ "Direct bookings are a source of above-average ADR for both hotel sites and incur low or zero customer acquisition costs. A customer loyalty scheme which encourages previous customers to book again will generate a greater booking volume of a higher ADR/low acquisition cost nature, which would improve profitability".

- Under "Seasonal Pricing", create a bulleted list and an initial recommendation.

○ "Both hotel sites, but particularly the Resort Hotel, have booking patterns and ADRs associated with a seasonal cycle. It is recommended that the business continue to price according to seasonal demand".

- Where we haven't made a recommendation under another title, it is because the analysis of ADR by Distribution Channel and Month hasn't revealed anything particularly relevant.
- Our document structure, with Analysis followed by Recommendations, is an example. In the real world, the analysis may be included as an appendix or not at all (for example, a slide show might just retain the thematic recommendations and not seek to justify them in the same space). These decisions would likely be guided by audience and context: a written report assumes the reader has longer to consider the information and can move through the content at their leisure.

The process by which we produced these charts to better explore and illustrate a hypothesis and then make recommendations based on some of the observed conclusions can be repeated. You will do this in the exercise's Challenge section below.

Exercise 14 – Challenge

In this challenge, you will repeat the process above, whereby you present a view of the data which supports one or more recommendations which you can include under a thematic subheading. Here are a few pointers:

- You should aim to include as few visualisations as required to make your point. Some of those produced during the exercise above will help to contextualise all other recommendations, so as you repeat this process for other analyses, you may need fewer and fewer visuals to justify your recommendations.
- You may choose one of your own analyses as the basis for recommendations in this challenge or use one of the two completed in Exercise 13 which have not yet been used (board basis and channel; party size and customer type).
- You may not be able to make recommendations under each heading—that's OK.
- Use the internet where required to better understand the industry or even the results of your analysis. Life is not a closed-book exam—making use of information from a wide variety of sources will improve your knowledge.

Add any new visualisations and observations to "Analysis & Observations" and any recommendations you can make to the associated thematic subheading (e.g., "Customer Segmentation").

Complete this process for two further analyses, investigating your initial PivotTable outputs with further analysis and visualisation and making recommendations based on your observations and supported by the visualisations you include.

Exercise 14 – Review

In this exercise, we used some of our exploratory data analysis from Exercise 13, which was limited to a summary table, to produce some visualisations that brought the data to life. These visualisations supported a number of recommendations to the Sales & Marketing Director. The recommendations were succinct and made reference to the analysis that supported them. The document produced was formatted in such a way that the reader could focus on the recommendations if they wished or take a closer look at the data itself to satisfy themselves that the recommendations were grounded in historical booking data.

The process which was followed looked like this:

- Analysis of business request.
- Exploratory data analysis based on initial hypotheses.
- Further analysis based on initial findings.
- Visualisation of further analyses to make clearer any relationships, differences, trends, threats and opportunities, creating insight.

- Recommendations based on observations from the insight, supported by the visualisations.

Remember, too, that one of our recommendations in this exercise was that further analysis be undertaken into customer profiles. You can't always find the answers the first time, and understanding the limitations of the data will help you define more realistic and nuanced recommendations.

EXERCISE 15

In this final exercise, you will consider two more business requests and complete the entire process from start to finish, including the analysis of the business request itself to determine where to start exploring. You may choose either request to explore:

1. What impact have cancelled bookings had on the business, and how might these be reduced in volume?
2. How valuable are agents in creating bookings for the business, and how might agent performance be improved?

Produce a report document in the style of the output from Exercise 14, which addresses one of these business questions.

Here are some tips to get you started:

- Search the internet to research the topic area. You are almost certain to find articles (possibly industry-specific) on mitigating and managing cancellations in business or on generating bookings and sales through 3rd parties. This will lead you to some initial hypotheses to explore.

- The process of exploratory data analysis and noting observations will help you pick the most promising areas for further analysis. Don't produce charts and recommendations from your first piece of exploratory work.

Exercise 15 – Challenge

There is no specific challenge for this exercise. However, challenge *yourself* in completing this exercise to try new things:

- Try chart types you haven't used before.
- Try new conditional formatting rules on summary data (e.g., flag values above or below a certain threshold).
- Create new columns in the dataset that support an analysis.
- Include any contextual data you find in your topic research that supports your recommendations (e.g., industry cancellation rates or the revenue share for agents in hotel bookings nationally).

Exercise 15 – Review

In completing Exercise 15, you have completed the final exercise of this book! We have slowly moved from describing exactly what you needed to do in each exercise to arrive at this point: where you have completed an end-to-end analysis of a business request yourself.

You also used the 3-step system described in this book:

- Prepare: determined what the problem is you are trying to solve, considered the data you had available and its limitations and, if needed, further developed the data to support some relevant analyses.
- Analyse: took the data and applied analytical techniques; first, to explore the data and make observations and then to refine these observations further.
- Consider: reflected on the business problem and audience to appropriately present your findings and make recommendations using the insight created.

CHAPTER SUMMARY/KEY TAKEAWAYS

We covered a lot in this chapter once again, and the exercises provided a greater opportunity to think through the business requests yourself and be more independent in producing exploratory analyses and generating your own conclusions from your observations.

As a reminder, we touched upon:

- The importance of your outputs addressing the problem statement in a manner suited to the audience.
- The value of contextual data such as industry metrics or

presenting performance in relation to organisational targets to answer the question, "so what"?

- How to analyse a broad business question by applying domain knowledge to develop an approach to your analysis and some starting hypotheses.
- How to explore your initial hypotheses and the value of recording observations.
- A practical application of revisiting the Prepare step to enhance the dataset to explore a hypothesis not served by the existing data ("Party Type").
- How to develop a written report containing business recommendations supported by Analysis & Observations.
- The process of curating a set of impactful visualisation to support the specific recommendations being made.
- Two new business requests for you to explore, giving you the chance to complete the entire process independently.

Your journey with this book could end here—however, it is recommended that you take the skills you have developed to this point and undertake a project of your own which will be introduced in the next chapter.

PART THREE
OVER TO YOU

In this final section of the book, we will introduce some next steps for you to take in your data analysis journey. The first of these is to undertake a project of your own which will involve sourcing your own dataset for analysis. We will then reflect on what remains to be learned in Microsoft Excel that is relevant to the data analyst role.

CHAPTER 9
COMPLETE A PROJECT

Undertaking a self-led data analysis project is an excellent way for someone learning data analysis to gain practical experience and develop their skills. Here are some of the benefits of doing so:

Hands-on experience: Working on a data analysis project provides further practical experience with real data, allowing you to apply the concepts and techniques you've learned in this book to another real-world problem.

Skill development: Completing a project will further develop your skills, including data cleaning, data development, data visualization, and analysis. Working on a self-led data analysis project will allow this to happen at your own pace and without any guidance.

Independent learning: Undertaking a self-led data analysis project requires a significant amount of independent learning, which can help to develop self-motivation and self-discipline.

Demonstrating skills to potential employers: Completing a self-led data analysis project can be a valuable addition to your resume or portfolio, demonstrating your ability to work with data and solve problems independently.

Personal interest: Undertaking a self-led data analysis project on a topic you are interested in can make the process more enjoyable and rewarding.

Overall, a self-led data analysis project is an excellent way to gain hands-on experience, develop your skills, demonstrate your abilities to potential employers, and pursue your personal interests in data analysis. If you are already working in a job role requiring these skills, you are well placed to start analysing data for your employer. If you are looking to change jobs, enter data analysis for the first time or are a student, then undertaking a project to demonstrate your ability is an excellent idea.

WHERE TO FIND DATA FOR YOUR PROJECT

This is probably the first question to ask yourself, as data representative of business systems can be hard to find. Most publicly available data is published by governments or researchers, and so is not representative of the *transactional* data of day-to-day business operations. That said, it can still be interesting and worth analysing.

The dataset for this project was found on Kaggle, a website for sharing data and analysis, primarily focused at data scientists. Here's a list of websites to consider:

Website	URL	Description
UCI Machine Learning Repository	https://archive.ics.uci.edu/ml/index.php	A collection of datasets for machine learning and data analysis covering various topics such as healthcare, finance, and social sciences.
Kaggle Datasets	https://www.kaggle.com/datasets	A repository of datasets covering a wide range of topics, including image recognition, natural language processing, and time series analysis.
Google Dataset Search	https://datasetsearch.research.google.com/	A search engine that indexes publicly available datasets, allowing users to search for datasets based on keywords or topics.
Data.gov	https://www.data.gov/	A repository of datasets provided by the US government, covering a range of topics such as climate, energy, and education.
FiveThirtyEight	https://data.fivethirtyeight.com/	Datasets related to current events and news topics, covering a range of topics such as politics, sports, and economics.

Try some of the links above and see if you can find anything either of personal interest or relevant to your current or future role. You may find that the data available is provided in formats that are not immediately accessible to Excel. Checking the file extension on a search engine may give you some clues as to how to open it—it may be that it is specifically encoded for a particular application, in which case you may have to source another file.

HOW TO STRUCTURE YOUR PROJECT

Having found some data that interests you, you will need to determine what to do next. It might be worth considering the following:

- Are you trying to impress a potential employer? Perhaps research the industry and determine some of the particular challenges involved in running a profitable business in this area. Consider how the data you have could inform the improved operation of the business and pose some business questions, which you then go on to solve.
- Are you trying to reinforce the skills learned in this book? You could imagine a similar set of business requests and produce some written reports and recommendations to a fictional director but for a new industry to encourage you to think afresh.
- Do you have a specific project to complete as part of a course or degree? Understand fully what your education provider requires you to demonstrate first and foremost, and then structure your analysis in such a way as to complete these objectives.

Remember that any data analysis should begin with a stated problem for resolution. Otherwise, you can spend a lot of time on exploratory analysis and get no further.

SHARING YOUR AWESOME ANALYSIS

Once you've completed your project, you can consider sharing it. This may be with a potential employer as part of a job application or for your own personal satisfaction! In business, it is common to use documents, slide shows, and spreadsheets to share information, so considering packaging your outputs this way will mean they can almost certainly be opened and accessed by the audience, but you will also demonstrate the ability to use these applications to effectively communicate.

You could also consider starting a blog or a personal website, which gives you complete creative freedom over how you wish to share your outputs. You could focus on the observations and insights created or on your personal journey with the analysis and the process you went through.

CHAPTER 10
WHAT NEXT?

The intention of this book was to introduce you to both Microsoft Excel and the art and practice of data analysis: in both cases, to take you from beginner to an intermediate level. As a result, you have learned many technical skills and application features, but there is more to learn!

Here is a list of things which were not covered in this book but may be the content of a future title:

- Tables and named ranges
- PivotCharts
- Sparklines
- Dashboards, slicers, timelines and interactive controls
- More advanced functions and statistics, such as forecasting
- Formula dependencies and error checking

- External data, connections and data models
- Workbook and worksheet protection
- Visual Basic for Applications (VBA)

Once you are happy that you have understood all the concepts in this book, can write your own formulas, use functions, analyse data and visualise it, you could certainly learn about some of the topics above and take your Excel to the next level.

It is also worth noting that the career of a data analyst will likely involve exposure to and the use of many more tools than Excel and require a knowledge of concepts such as database design and modelling (so that you can find the data you need within a system), business analysis (so that you can correctly interpret business requirements), performance management (so that you can help a business use data to improve its operations), and more. Among the technical skills that are of most use are SQL (Structured Query Language—allows you to retrieve data from systems) and a relevant business intelligence application such as Tableau, Power BI, Business Objects, and so on (other packages are available). Ultimately, you may also need to learn a programming language such as Python.

That said, a range of roles exist within the domain of data analysis, and you don't have to become ever more technical and specialised to create a successful and satisfying career for your-self. Being able to interpret data, not just retrieve and summarise it, is an incredibly valuable skill to a business, and it has been an intention of this book that you learn the value of *applied knowledge* and not just technical skill. In this way, we hope the book has given you something not often found online by combining technical skills with the art and practice of analysis.

Good luck. See you in the next book. If you enjoyed this book, please share your experience with others and leave a review wherever you bought it.

THANK YOU FOR READING!

I hope you found "Data Analysis in Microsoft Excel" helpful and that it has enhanced your skills and knowledge. Your feedback is incredibly valuable to me and helps other readers make informed decisions.

If you enjoyed this book or found it useful, please consider leaving a review wherever you bought it. Your honest review will not only help me improve future editions but also assist others in discovering valuable resources for their learning journey.

Here's how you can leave an Amazon review:

1. Visit the book's page on Amazon.
2. Scroll down to the "Customer Reviews" section.
3. Click on the "Write a customer review" button.
4. Share your thoughts and experiences.

Or follow this QR code:

Thank you for your support and happy analyzing!

Best regards,

   - Alex Holloway

JOIN MY MAILING LIST!

If you are interested in future titles, please consider joining my mailing list. This includes opportunities to access books and resources before they are published for FREE as I am always interested in feedback and reviews on new releases.

Follow the QR code below to sign up for these exclusive opportunities. You may unsubscribe at any time:

NOTES

INTRODUCTION

1. https://techjury.net/blog/how-much-data-is-created-every-day/.
2. https://www.statista.com/statistics/871513/worldwide-data-created/.

3. THE 3-STEP SYSTEM IN DATA ANALYSIS

1. https://www.qlik.com/us/data-analytics/data-insights.

5. THE PROJECT

1. Hotel booking demand datasets. Data in Brief, Volume 22, 2019, Pages 41-49, ISSN 2352-3409, https://doi.org/10.1016/j.dib.2018.11.126.

6. PREPARE

1. https://www.iso.org/iso-3166-country-codes.html .

8. CONSIDER

1. A business effectively 'pays' for new customers by way of its spend on advertising, branding, staff working in sales/account management, commissions to agents and tour operators etc.
2. See formal definitions at sciencedirect.com link where dataset was found for further notes.
3. https://insights.ehotelier.com/insights/2015/06/16/website-gds-and-ota-the-right-mix-in-distribution-channel-investments/.

BIBLIOGRAPHY

Lotame, "What Are the Methods of Data Collection?, May 13, 2019, https://www.lotame.com/what-are-the-methods-of-data-collection/

Adi Bhat, QuestionPro.com, "Data Collection: What It Is, Methods & Tools + Examples", https://www.questionpro.com/blog/data-collection/

Coursera, "What Is Data Analysis? (With Examples)", February 23, 2023, https://www.coursera.org/articles/what-is-data-analysis-with-examples

Ajitesh Kumar, VitalFlux.com, "Hypothesis Testing Steps & Examples", March 4, 2023, https://vitalflux.com/data-science-how-to-formulate-hypothesis-for-hypothesis-testing/

Nathan Yau, BigThink.com, "Understanding Data – Context", June 28, 2013, https://bigthink.com/articles/understanding-data-context/

Microsoft, "Top ten ways to clean your data", https://support.microsoft.com/en-us/office/top-ten-ways-to-clean-your-data-2844b620-677c-47a7-ac3e-c2e157d1db19

Kristen Bialik, Capterra.com, "What Is Contextual Data and How to Collect It", June 25, 2019, https://www.capterra.com/resources/how-to-collect-contextual-data/

Treehouse Technology Group, "Understanding the Difference Between Data, Information and Business Insights", https://treehousetechgroup.com/understanding-the-difference-between-data-information-and-business-insights/

eHotelier, "Website, GDS and OTA: the right mix in distribution channel investments", June 16, 2015, https://insights.ehotelier.com/insights/2015/06/16/website-gds-and-ota-the-right-mix-in-distribution-channel-investments/

Laura Fredericks, Cvent, "The Complete Guide to Hotel Distribution Channels", May 20, 2021, https://www.cvent.com/en/blog/hospitality/hotel-distribution-channels

ABOUT THE AUTHOR

Alex Holloway is an experienced data professional with over 15 years' experience across multiple industries in both public and private sectors. He has worked as both an employee and consultant during this time and is passionate about finding valuable information and insight in data and sharing this with others.

Having used multiple data technologies (past and present) and systems, his varied experience has allowed him to condense this broad knowledge into a set of general principles which can be applied in any context. This experience has also highlighted the value of both soft skills and technical skills to the effective analyst: a principle reflected throughout this book in the approach taught to analysing data.

Alex lives in the United Kingdom and continues to work as a consultant and author.